Nicholas

Rarely Ordinary Time
Some Memoirs

Rarely Ordinary Time

Some Memoirs

of the Right Reverend Nicholas Reade.
Edited for publication by Dr. Richard Ralph.

*"To Christine who has shared so much
of the journey, and to all those
I have ministered with."*

All profit from the memoirs will be donated to the
work of **Bladder Cancer Research** and the
Additional Curates Society which helps to
finance priests in many of our poorest parishes.

First published in the UK 2019
© Nicholas Reade, 2019

This book has been printed by Rother Print.
2b Amherst Road, Bexhill-on-Sea TN40 1QJ.

ISBN: 978-1-5272-4282-1

Copies available from various locations
and from 5, Warnham Gardens, Bexhill-on-Sea
TN39 3SP 01424 842673
nicholas.reade@btinternet.com

CONTENTS

*Driving a Blackpool tram. Passengers include
Archbishop Rowan.*

FOREWORD

This began as a small book along similar lines to one my mother wrote some thirty years ago for the family and close friends. My good friend, the Revd. Dr. Richard Ralph, former Principal of Westminster College, Oxford suggested that in view of the varied ministry I had exercised over forty-six years there might be wider interest. He also thought that those on the Catholic wing of the Church of England might be interested to hear from someone who, from an early age, embraced Anglo-Catholicism, and has remained consistent in his position in times of very significant change. As most of my ministry has been in parishes, and my heart has always been with the parish and people, Fr. Richard felt many parishioners and clergy might also be interested. We also wondered if this might also be of interest more widely. Whilst my ecclesiological conviction has always been clear, I hope I am not seen as partisan. I have, with ease and joy, always worked across the broad spectrum of the Church of England – and with other denominations – and have made many friends throughout the whole Church.

I am thankful to God for every phase of my life, and for calling me to serve as a priest in His Church. I thank Him for my family, for the sacrifices my parents made, for close friends, colleagues and all those I have had the privilege of ministering with and to. In a short book like this this I cannot possibly mention everyone I would like to. I am conscious that I have omitted many key people who have made a deep impression on me and encouraged me. This omission in no way minimises my gratitude to them all.

As I am essentially a parish priest, I have tried in these pages to give the beginnings of an answer to the questions I have often been asked, 'What is a priest?' and 'What do you do?' – and to do so by providing a broad summary of my journey so far, and particularly as a priest and bishop in the Church of God, with some indicative detail. This is most certainly not an attempt to write a detailed and scholarly episcopal memoir which we often read in the past – rather it offers just a glimpse of life as a priest throughout a little over the last quarter of the twentieth, and much of the first quarter of the twenty-first, centuries. I was most anxious to complete this while there are still a good number of those who have made much of this journey alongside me, especially members of earlier congregations I served.

I am particularly grateful to Dr. Ralph for his wisdom and the many hours he has given to helping me with this, and for his friendship, and also to Mrs Karen Jones who has given invaluable work in preparing the manuscript for the printing process. Karen, with her husband Fr. Alan (1947-2018) has been a great friend for many years. I am indebted also to Meg Davies from Preston in the Blackburn Diocese who has provided the index and checked the manuscript, and as always, for my wife, Christine, who has supported me throughout, and shared so much of it all.

+ Nicholas
The Epiphany of the Lord, 2019

1   EARLY YEARS

At the time of my birth (9 December 1946) my father was serving in the Royal Air Force, stationed at RAF Aldergrove in Northern Ireland; my mother had to make a rough crossing from Larne to Stranraer and then travelled to the South Coast so that I could be born in a nursing home in Bexhill, where my grandparents lived, and where we spent my very early years. I had an elder brother, Jeremy, who was five years old, and a sister, Gillian, who was only eleven months and ten days older than me. I was to receive two family names, Stewart and Sturrock, but my parents had not decided on a first name. It was the Matron of the Nursing Home, at 11 De La Warr Road, who suggested 'Nicholas', as it was three days after the Feast of St. Nicholas. I am not sure whether I would have been called Mary if I had been a girl, as the day before my birth was the Festival of the Immaculate Conception of the Blessed Virgin Mary.

Strangely, I was not baptised until 1948 - on another Marian Festival, 15 August. The Assumption of the Blessed Virgin Mary was not promulgated as a dogma in the Latin Church until three years later, and the Church of England had to wait until 2000 to celebrate 15 August as The Festival of the Blessed Virgin Mary. My father told me that I started talking very early, and he remembered that on the morning of my baptism at St. Mark's Church, Little Common, I was enquiring 'When are we going to the God Shop?' On carrying out my first visitation to this church as Archdeacon of Lewes and Hastings some forty-nine years later, the vicar greeted me with the baptismal register and pointed out the entry. In retirement I sometimes celebrate the Eucharist at St. Mark's, where the font, at the far west end of the church, is directly aligned with the altar; as the celebrant says the words 'Let us give thanks to the Lord our God', I give thanks to God for my life in Christ beginning at that font.

We had two homes during our time in Little Common, with my father travelling to the Air Ministry in London by train six days a week. My first school was a kindergarten with the name 'Mayfield' on the edge of Bexhill which my sister and I attended. In my late teens I told a priest I had been to Mayfield Kindergarten, and he mentioned that there was a delightful village in Sussex called Mayfield, with a beautiful church dating back to Saxon times and an Anglo-Catholic tradition. I was to become the vicar there from 1982 to 1988.

I remember sitting in the back of our Austin 7 with my sister as we drove past St. Mark's, Little Common in 1951, at a time when there was much activity at the church; my Mother told us it was General Election Day and valiantly tried to explain to us the purpose of a General Election. Two days later as we drove past the church again, on our way to our grandparents, I asked who had won, and she was overjoyed to tell me that it was Mr Churchill. Always inquisitive, I said, 'What about Mr Attlee?' and she said, 'He got it all wrong!' I remember feeling sorry for him - as I did for Hugh Gaitskell eight years later when I was at preparatory school – by then I had begun to understand that Mr Attlee had in fact been a great reforming Prime Minister, who created the NHS and established the welfare state.

1939 - My grandmother, Gertrude Fleming, my uncle, Gordon Fleming, my mother, Eileen.

In 1952 my father was appointed Commanding Officer of the RAF Unit in the Hook of Holland. We lived in a house that had been the local German headquarters during the War. My sister and I spent endless hours trying to break into the German safe in our bedroom, and when my brother was back from boarding school in Bexhill, he had no greater success.

My sister, Gillian, and I attended the local British Forces Education Service School where Mrs Murphy and Miss Freans gave us a good basic education in a Nissen hut. We were quite privileged in our quarters with a 'batman' and a Dutch maid, and a RAF driver would pick us up for school. Manners and good behaviour were drummed into us by our parents - one of my very first serious punishments came after I pulled the driver's hat off.

Stupidly, I chose to do this within sight of our house, and my mother enquired why the car had stopped so abruptly at the end of the road. While I was often in trouble for playing the fool (especially when my brother was at home, goading me on) it was very out of character for me to treat those who cared for us without respect. I always made friends with them, and the 'maids' were keen to invite me to their homes to tea. Some years later, when I was eight, I recall going to tea with the 'daily help' in Coltishall. Even at that age I was shocked to discover that people lived in houses with a lavatory at the end of the garden which was emptied once a week – and I happened to be there on the sixth day.

We attended church every Sunday on the RAF Station in the Hook of Holland, and afterwards went to the

Officers' Mess for sherry and orange juice. (It was there that I first saw a programme on television, the Coronation service of the present Queen.) I recall that the Sunday Service - which was sometimes a Parade Service - was pretty middle-of-the-road Matins, but I later encountered other padres who had caught the vision of the Parish Communion Movement, and even some with an Anglo-Catholic background.

One Sunday I was very puzzled. I liked my father's Warrant Officer, but he was waiting outside another Nissen hut almost opposite the Anglican church. I waved to him, and then asked my parents why he did not come to church with us, and what was 'this church' he went to. I was told that he was a member of the Roman Catholic Church, which followed the Pope and 'worshipped' the Blessed Virgin Mary. Once again, as with Mr Attlee, I wanted to know more. Why was he wrong too? Indeed, why was he in some way the 'underdog'?

The RAF and the army in the Hook of Holland worked closely together, and my parents became friendly with the army doctor and his wife, Herbie and Maybeth - who were to keep in touch with my parents for the rest of their lives. What I did not know until after I began my ministry as Bishop of Blackburn, was that Maybeth was outside the cathedral standing to my left on the day of my installation and enthronement. She watched on as I hammered on the cathedral's west door with the Saxon Hammer, which every Bishop of Blackburn has used to gain entry on the day of his enthronement.

In July 1954 we returned to the UK on a troop ship, spending the rest of the summer in Bexhill with my grandparents, my aunt and uncle, and my cousins who had come back from Nairobi; during that long, hot summer other members of the family came down to spend time in Bexhill. Most mornings we went to Bexhill beach to my grandmother's beach hut, and most afternoons to Cooden Beach using another family beach hut. Not much variety there! With the arrival of September, the time was rapidly approaching for me to 'be a man' even though I was only seven-and-three-quarters. Childhood was expected to be brief, and the pace of 'growing up' somewhat forced.

My parents went off to my father's next posting, RAF Coltishall, near Norwich, and I went as a boarder to Sandown School in Hastings Road, Bexhill. It was described as a 'Home School for Little Boys and Girls'. Only those who were in the very bottom dormitory (five and six year-olds) were allowed to take teddy bears to bed, but I used to smuggle my little brown bear in.

While I made friends there, I did not do very well. The Headmaster and his sister were very sporty, but I did not excel at sport at any stage. Corporal punishment was another reality of school life – I recall one summer's morning, when I was aged nine and we were making a little noise at 6.30 in the dormitory, the Headmaster came in and beat us all with his dog's lead. I was unlucky enough to get the side with the studs on, but because I was growing up 'to be a man' I managed not to let anyone see me crying.

Near R.A.F. Coltishall in 1955. My parents,
my sister, Gillian and brother, Jeremy.

Every Sunday morning, we went to St. Michael's, Glassenbury Drive, and were crammed in with Ancaster House, Ancaster Gate, and Charters Towers Schools. Only once was the service anything other than Matins - I think it must have been a Eucharist of Requiem on Remembrance Sunday, because the priest wore black vestments. We were all quite excited by this change of service and asked questions afterwards.

So, by the age of ten, I had learnt to spell well, I had learnt my tables, I knew some Latin, and could box, and - eventually - swim; but above all I had learnt to survive boarding school life. I was therefore prepared for my next boarding school, Normandale, in Collington Avenue, Bexhill, which my brother had attended earlier. I felt at home immediately. The Headmaster was a good communicator and very jolly; he spent any profit on the Chapel and on maintaining the sports facilities. So good was the cricket field that the Sussex County team even played there once.

I could not believe my eyes on the first Sunday morning in Chapel, when we were given a service book with the title 'Mass' on the front. Everyone made the sign of the Cross. The priest entered clothed in gold vestments and wearing a biretta, a gong sounded during the Eucharistic Prayer. This was worship that came alive for me. And we were allowed to get up early on Wednesdays and major Saints' Days to attend early - morning Mass. Those being prepared for confirmation had to go to confession. There were photos of the Chapel being consecrated by the Bishop of Mauritius some ten years previously.

While I instinctively knew all that went on in the Chapel was as it should be, I was puzzled. My father was a member of the Church of Ireland but it appeared to me that he had sent me to a Roman Catholic School; I spoke to the French Master, Mr Hockley, who explained that we were Anglo-Catholic, and while there were other expressions in the Church of England, this was the right one. Strangely, when I was told, 'we were right', I chose to accept it. More excitement was in store when we went to the chaplain's parish, All Saints Sidley, the local Anglo-Catholic Church; here, with a flickering candle light beside it, the Blessed Sacrament was reserved in a beautiful domed Tabernacle - everyone genuflected in front of it, and there was always the lingering smell of incense. When the chaplain was ill for a period, the Archdeacon of Hastings, Guy Mayfield, usually came to celebrate Mass. We liked him because he told us stories in the sacristy before Mass - on one occasion he told us that he had driven on the Preston by-pass (in the Diocese of Blackburn) at 80 m.p.h. How strange that thirty-seven years later I would succeed him as Archdeacon. (Guy had been a RAF chaplain during the war; a diary of his ministry in 1939-41 serving on active Fighter Command Stations has recently been published by the Trustees of the Imperial War Museum, as *Life and Death in the Battle of Britain*, 2018.)

Normandale School is long gone, but I have returned to All Saints again and again throughout my life, and I concelebrated Mass on the fortieth anniversary of my ordination to the priesthood there with three former diocesan bishops of 'The Society.' It is a joy and huge privilege to serve there in a small way in retirement. On the indices of multiple deprivation, it is one of the poorest areas in the country.

While there were a couple of odd masters at Normandale, one of whom was asked to move on, and I suspect today would have been interviewed by the Police, it was a happy and friendly school. If we had seriously transgressed, the only corporal punishment we received was a mild beating from the Headmaster with a miniature cricket bat autographed by the 1948 England Test Team. We had our own swimming pool and were well fed - I still remember the delicious sausages.

All boys were prepared for the Common Entrance Examination. As a result of a holiday in the summer of 1959 in Guernsey, where my uncle Mervyn was Master-in-Charge of Elizabeth College Prep School, it was decided I would go to Elizabeth College in the Michaelmas Term 1960. I was given the choice of attending Dean Close, Cheltenham or Elizabeth College. We had enjoyed Guernsey for three weeks that summer, and Guernsey also had the advantage of an aunt and uncle to have me out on exeat; so, in September 1960, my father, who was at that time Chief Instructor at the RAF Administrative Apprentices Training School, Bircham Newton, drove me down to the school train at Waterloo where I met up with other boarders to travel to Weymouth and to board the night boat to Guernsey.

The main piece of advice my father had given me in the car, was that if any senior boy 'tried anything on', or started bullying me, to punch him on the nose so he got tears in his eyes and the other boys would start laughing at him. So with a firm hand shake, and looking him fixedly in the eye and keeping the tears at bay, I boarded the school train on my next step to 'becoming a man'. There was not much bullying at Elizabeth College, although the prefects were allowed to beat - and did; the Housemaster, Major Manchester, who was generally a kind man, caned quite freely, but sometimes he suspected he was beating a carpet - for we would put plenty of layers of padding on.

Life was pretty tough. There was a short run every

morning followed by a shower. If it was raining we were excused the run and had a cold shower instead, and everything was overseen by a prefect, to ensure we stayed under the shower long enough. After lessons there would be sport on Mondays, and on Tuesdays the whole afternoon was given over to the Combined Cadet Force (CCF) parade - we were allowed into the town in our corps uniform afterwards. On Wednesdays and Thursdays after lessons, if not down for games, we could go out cycling – in that case we had to report en-route, in an attempt to prevent our getting 'up to no good', which we usually did anyway. On Fridays after school once a fortnight we had CCF again, although this time we did not have to change into full army uniform. On the other Friday we had Activities and Societies, and I usually joined the Debating Society. We had Saturday morning chapel and lessons, and usually sport in the afternoon.

On Sundays there was formal Matins in the School Chapel – which also served as the Parish Church of St. James the Less - and we would always use the Book of Common Prayer (1662) and the Public School Hymn Book. Perhaps what made life a bit tougher for the sixty-five boarders in School House was that we were a minority, and of course subjected to the full rigours of mid-twentieth-century public school boarding life. Once a fortnight we were allowed out on exeat after Sunday chapel, and I am everlastingly grateful to my aunt and uncle and two cousins, David and Joanna, for all their kindness and generosity; they always gave me a good time and fed me well - and even gave me a proper drink when I reached sixteen.

I have kept in touch with the School, and was invited in 2003 to be Guest-of-Honour at the Old Elizabethan Dinner, the day after I had received the letter from the Prime Minister asking me to be Bishop of Blackburn - of course, I couldn't whisper a word about that to anybody. I returned in 2008 to present prizes at the school. On another occasion, when I was over to preach for the Island Liberation Day, Bishop Michael Scott-Joynt of Winchester asked me to ordain to the priesthood a contemporary of mine at the College, the Revd. John Luff, in the local parish church, with another contemporary preaching; the reception afterwards was held in the Great Hall of the College.

I was not confirmed at Normandale School, so in my first year at Elizabeth College I went to the chaplain's confirmation classes, and then missed the confirmation, as I had to have an operation in the RAF hospital at Ely at the time of the Bishop's visit. While in hospital there were some stirrings in my inner life. I went to the hospital chapel and was touched by a sermon from an ordinand at Ely Theological College, and he chatted with me afterwards. When confirmation preparation came round the next year, I told the chaplain I didn't need to attend his classes again, but he insisted I did - and how right he was.

This time I took the course more seriously, asked a lot of questions - especially as to why the services were not like those in the chapel at Normandale and at All Saints' Sidley. I appreciated the care given to us in preparation by the Revd. Ralph Scrine (who, I discovered, had been called Father Scrine in his previous posts); after we made our first Holy Communion, on the Sunday following the confirmation, he gave us the little book, *In His Presence,* which I still have. I came to appreciate that it was an excellent 'Prayer-Book Catholic' publication, helping to prepare the newly confirmed for the next stage of their journey of faith. For many years I too gave candidates the book. The confirming bishop was Dr. Faulkner Alison, Bishop of Winchester and the Visitor to the College. In 1973 and 1974 he went to the trouble of finding out where my two ordination retreats were, and sent a personally-written letter to me on each occasion. However, I gained the impression that the focus on our confirmation day was less on the bishop and more on the famous broadcaster Richard Dimbleby who was godfather to one of the candidates.

I was now fifteen, and started to think what I might be and do after school, and it seemed to me that the few gifts I had could best be used as a priest. I went to see the headmaster, Mr. Day, who was a reader and lay minister, and who was taking me for divinity that year. I did not expect much encouragement as I had been in trouble from time to time. He once told the chaplain, 'There's no bad in the boy, but he does some extraordinary things.' At that time, I had actually just written an essay on Amos for the principal, and he said it was the best piece of work I had produced for him and it showed signs of promise. He was generous and encouraging, and remained so from that day. Indeed, he was absurdly generous when I went to bid him farewell on the day I departed, when he said, 'You have had an excellent career here.'

I had decided that if I was to be a priest I had to be totally committed, and to me at that time I could only see this being worked through by taking my boyhood Anglo-Catholic position seriously. There would be a tension here, for that was not the official position of the school, and with my new-found zeal I asked the chaplain if I could start going to St. Stephen's, the Anglo-Catholic Church on the edge of St. Peter Port, on at least one Sunday a month. His advice was sound, although I did not altogether appreciate it at the time; he warned me against an attachment to ceremonial in our worship, and then added, 'perhaps it would be better if we had a Sung Eucharist here once a month'.

On Pentecost that year he had persuaded the headmaster that it would be right to have a full Sung Eucharist with vestments and four servers once a month. He and Mr. Day had begun to talk about the kind of churches the boys might attend for worship after they had left school. In reality, a lot of them would go nowhere, but the pattern emerged that once a month there would be a Parish Communion, once a month a Sung Eucharist, and twice a month Matins. Even so, I managed to go to Solemn Evensong at St. Stephen's and the occasional High Mass, and I made my first confession to Canon Kemp, the vicar, and went to confession regularly - I owe much to him from this very formative period. I am also grateful to him for introducing me to Fr. Martin Jarrett-Kerr of the Community of the Resurrection (CR), who was in Guernsey preaching for a week; Martin invited me to stay at the Community's London House at the end of

the Michaelmas term - and so began my association
with the CR.

My debt to Ralph, the chaplain, is very great. I was
young and hot-headed - confident that I was right, and
that Anglo-Catholicism would 'conquer' the whole of
the Anglican Communion. Ralph was the best kind
of Liberal Catholic, although ministering in a school
with 'middle of the road' churchmanship. He was
prayerful, disciplined, wise, gentle and a clear thinker,
always picking up on the best points you had made and
suggesting ways of progress. He could see things were
changing in the Church more widely, not least that the
wind of the Second Vatican Council, then in session,
was also blowing our way. Ralph had been curate
to that great high-church left-wing prelate, Mervyn
Stockwood, who went on to be Bishop of Southwark.
One of the other curates was John Robinson, later
Bishop of Woolwich, who was to become the popular
face of New Theology, shaking the country with the
publication of *Honest to God* in March 1963.

Ralph therefore appreciated and shared much of
my understanding of worship and of the life of the
Church, but he did not want me to become narrow,
so he encouraged me to read *Honest to God*, and
gave me a copy of Mervyn Stockwood's *Cambridge
Sermons* and a couple of books written by Joost de
Blank, Archbishop of Capetown. He was pleased
that I had started thinking more deeply about social
issues, speaking out against apartheid and poverty at
meetings. The agenda put forward by the new Leader

of the Opposition, Harold Wilson, seemed to chime with me, particularly with its emphasis on tackling poverty, unemployment, low pay and racism. I kept in touch with Fr. Ralph until his death at the age of ninety-eight in the autumn of 2017, and was privileged to take part in his funeral rites.

A number of my contemporaries have kept in touch since we left Elizabeth College more than fifty years ago – indeed, I was humbled to have friends from school at my installation in Blackburn Cathedral and when I made my maiden speech in the House of Lords in 2009. In the Houses of Parliament I was especially pleased to be reunited with my exact contemporary, Malcolm Wicks. Malcolm had become Labour MP for one of the Croydon constituencies and was a popular Member. Even when Labour went out of power in 2010, Malcolm bucked the trend and increased his majority. Among his other appointments in Government, 1997-2010, Malcolm was Minister of State in four departments. In his autobiography, he recalls during his schooldays how he and I would walk down the road on a Friday, he to collect the left-wing political weekly *Tribune* and me to pick up *The Church Times*.

I had lunch in the Commons with Malcolm and another contemporary shortly before I left Blackburn, and he told us he was losing weight because he was on 'the Marsden diet' – his way of signalling that he was dying of cancer. There were very few at the College who were not 'true blue' and I was sorry that Malcolm left before the General Election in 1964, when we had a proper school election, overseen by one of the junior housemasters, Bruce Parker (who went on to become a journalist and television presenter). Malcolm's departure meant that I had to be the Labour candidate, although considerably further to the right than he. At the beginning of the campaign, Bruce told me that if I won I would be interviewed on Channel Television. That was not to be - nevertheless, I consider that to have polled over fifty votes in an Independent School on a very conservative island, at that time, was quite an achievement.

While strict discipline was maintained at Elizabeth College, certain things began to change between 1963 and 1965. We were able go out a little more without constant supervision, and there was a more relaxed approach to events which included girls - especially those from Blanchelande Convent School. My lifelong friend, Beverley McKay (*née* Webber), was an Anglican, and used to come to the school chapel on occasions with her aunt Lily, whose house provided a safe haven in which we could meet convent girls. Recently I learnt from another long-time friend, Norma Williams (*née* Renier), who was head girl at the time, that the Reverend Mother rang up the headmaster one day and began the conversation, 'Mr. Day I want to talk to you about sex'. That was the start of some joint social events for us, the last of which took place on the island in October 2015, fifty years after we left our respective schools.

My father had been posted to RAF Stafford while I was at Elizabeth College; during one Christmas vacation I ventured into St. James' Church in the neighbouring village of Salt. I could not believe that, so near to home, and deep in the country, was a church with 'full Catholic privileges'. Father Warrington, the parish priest, showed me around and asked if I would like to serve some weekday Masses when I was at home. I eagerly accepted the invitation - and there was always a cooked breakfast with him in the Vicarage afterwards. He had two daughters, who were at the Convent School in Stafford; and the younger one, Veronica, became my first 'serious' girlfriend. We kept in touch until she died, in 2010, and I conducted the commendation and farewell at her Funeral Mass in St. Chad's Stafford - having earlier participated there in the funeral rites for both her parents.

Father Warrington was an old-fashioned Anglo-Catholic priest who seemed to know everybody and had a solution for every problem; he gave rise to much amusement, and even now hardly a day goes by when we do not imitate one of his many mannerisms. He treated me like an extension to the family, but I can never forget the huge encouragement he gave to me – he was a deep well of pastoral wisdom, and in so many ways a role model.

In the early - to mid-sixties not many young people went to university; while there were foundation scholarships at Oxbridge colleges for Elizabeth College boys, such aspirations were out of my league, and I have to confess I did not work hard for 'A' levels. While I was confident that I had the beginnings of a vocation to the priesthood, I accepted that after eleven years of boarding school – which had helped me to become a 'real man' - I still needed to give myself a year out before deciding which path I should follow to ordination. Confirmation that I was a 'real man' came when there was a sherry party at home, and my father took me to one side and enquired whether I would like a 'man's sherry' – and not to draw attention to the fact I was drinking anything different he put a Bushmills Whiskey in a sherry glass.

2   THE NEXT STEP

In some respects this 'gap year' was a difficult time. I
lived at home, in the Staffordshire countryside, with my
parents. My father had retired from the regular Royal
Air Force, and taken a post as Wing Administrative
Officer for the Staffordshire Wing Air Training Corps
with his headquarters at RAF Stafford. He finally
retired in 1980. Apart from holidays, I had not lived
at home since I was seven; from time to time there was
tension with my parents, and I did not find it easy. I
was missing my friends from school, being a prefect - 'a
big fish in a small pond' - and the settled community
life of the boarding house.

I found a job as a clerical assistant in the District
Valuer's office in Stafford, travelling to work by bus with
my trilby and rolled umbrella. (By an extraordinary
coincidence, the bus driver – a man called Cyril –
turned up seven years later as the driver of the bus
which took me from the Retreat House to Lichfield
Cathedral on the day of my priestly ordination.) I was
not 'stretched' in the valuation office, but made plenty
of friends, socialising with staff out of office hours,
drinking too much, and generally having a good time.

During this time, I also helped to run a local youth
club, producing a couple of plays for them, and
organising an 'Any Questions' evening. I managed
to put together a good panel, which included a
bishop, a consultant psychiatrist, the head teacher of
a comprehensive school, and the Arts Minister, Jennie

Lee (the widow of Nye Bevan, the creator of the NHS). In the interval, Jennie said, 'I know the name of that psychiatrist, but I can't remember why.' I was able to remind her that his brother had stood against her in the 1964 General Election. Six years later, in an unexpected election result, Jennie lost the seat to a local schoolmaster, Patrick Cormack, someone for whom I have always had great respect. Patrick was a keen and devout churchman, fighting for many years to maintain traditional orthodoxy in the Church of England. I was pleased to encounter him again twenty-five years later, in the General Synod, and then in the House of Lords, when we used to meet to discuss matters of common interest.

Soon after I started working as a lowly civil servant, I went to Lichfield to see Canon Dudley Hodges, the Director of Ordinands; we agreed that with just two modest 'A' level passes, I would apply to go the following September to Christ Church College, Canterbury where my old school chaplain had become a lecturer. Upon completion of the course I would teach for a couple of years before proceeding to theological college. A few months before I was due to go to Canterbury, again visiting Canon Hodges, he advised me to decline the place at Canterbury and to read for a degree. This would mean brushing up my 'A' levels in the coming academic year. In the event, following immediate interview, the Community of the Resurrection offered me a place on their Qualifying Candidates' Scheme at the Hostel of the Resurrection in Leeds. If all went well I would then enrol at Leeds University the following September.

In those days the College of the Resurrection had a four-term year and was in full session when I arrived for interview. I will never forget entering the Community Church for the first time and attending High Mass on Sunday morning. I immediately felt that this was where I belonged. Fr. Eric Simmons, the Warden of the Hostel of the Resurrection, interviewed me, with Fr. Edward Symonds, the senior brother in the Community (who was also a tutor at the Hostel), and a Doctor of Divinity at the University of Oxford; and Fr. Aidan Mayoss, a very out-going, bouncy priest who later represented the northern religious communities with distinction in General Synod. They agreed that I should have a place, but I could not start until three weeks after term began, as I had to work out my notice in the civil service.

I arrived on a wet Saturday evening at the Hostel of the Resurrection, in Springfield Mount, Leeds, just as the Angelus bell was ringing at the start of Solemn Evensong. Fortunately, there was a paying guest, John Rodwell, in the entrance hall to greet me. John was a botanist, later to be ordained and to serve in parochial ministry. He became Professor of Ecology at Lancaster University and Honorary Canon of Blackburn Cathedral. During my time in the diocese, he was awarded the President's Medal by the Institute for Ecology and Environmental Management. So John, who was later one of 'my' clergy, and would be at my final Eucharist in Blackburn Cathedral exactly forty-six years later, looked after me for half-an-hour at the very beginning of my preparation for ordination.

I was somewhat surprised to notice a young woman in the midst of the first group of students who appeared on the stairs after Evensong, having been informed that no women were ever allowed in the Hostel; it transpired that women could come to Solemn Evensong on Saturdays. They sat on their own in the Lady Chapel and looked at us singing Evensong – and were entertained afterwards in the New Room, opposite the Warden's Office. I was later told that the young woman I saw was Christine Jasper, who was reading theology at Leeds University. Christine was the daughter of Canon Ronald Jasper, Reader in liturgical studies at King's College, London and a former Mirfield student; he had recently succeeded the Archbishop of York as Chairman of the Church of England Liturgical Commission. Nearly five years later, Christine and I were married in Westminster Abbey, where her father was, by then, a Residentiary Canon of the Abbey.

I felt at home straightaway at the Hostel (as I had done in the Community); I loved the daily routine and made friends with no trouble. Initially some of my contemporaries saw me as a bit of a curiosity: a public school boy who arrived in a coat with a velvet collar, sometimes sported a bow tie and used a cigarette holder. It was decided that I should retake my 'A' Level in History and also take 'A' level Religious Studies – however I was allowed to substitute 'A' level Politics for Religious Studies, working by correspondence course. This way of studying was new to me, but I read keenly and always completed the weekly essay - and to my surprise, after only six months, was awarded an A grade. With Politics, an improved History result, and my existing English 'A' level, I was qualified to matriculate.

All but three of the students at the Hostel were either candidates for ordination or aspiring ordinands. Sixty-five percent were already in the University, and most would proceed to the College of the Resurrection, twelve miles away at Mirfield, upon graduation for two or three years of final preparation for ordination. The Hostel of the Resurrection was a little like a Junior Seminary and had been built at the very beginning of the twentieth century to provide a university education for those hoping to be ordained whose parents could not afford the fees. Initially it had been a five-year course, three spent at the Hostel and two at the College at Mirfield.

At the Hostel we lived alongside six brethren of the Community of the Resurrection. The basic rule of life for students included Mass at 7.15am on at least five days a week - additionally we could join the brethren for Matins and Prime at 6.45pm - Evensong every day, and half an hour's silent meditation. Sometimes one of the brethren might say a 'private' Mass at 6.05am, and, if we were down to serve that, we would proudly tell everyone we were 'on the six-five special' (which was at that time a Saturday night pop programme with DJ Pete Murray). We were each assigned one of the priest brethren as our spiritual director and confessor. There were strict silence rules. If we went out of the building on a weekday evening, we had to be in by 10.00pm (or 10.30pm on Saturdays). If we transgressed any rule, we were expected to report it to the Warden on Saturday morning after the special weekly devotional address in Chapel. Sometimes there was a large queue.

The Church of the Resurrection and Mother House of the Community of the Resurrection at Mirfield, West Yorkshire.

After my qualifying year, the Community ceased to take pre-matriculation candidates, and the Hostel of the Resurrection became a hall of residence of the university, giving preferential places to those training for ordination. This meant, of course, that we were not all able to live under a common rule of life. Sadly, nine years later, the Hostel of the Resurrection was sold to the university, and a unique form of pre-theological college formation was lost to the Church of

England. At about the same time, other residential pre-theological courses closed, including Kelham, which was also run by a monastic order. This was a great loss for those who lacked the necessary qualifications for university or theological-college entrance – and it was the end of a scheme that offered an excellent spiritual formation, endowed with the blessings that come from living in community, learning, praying and growing together. Many of us owed much to the life at the Hostel, and I am truly grateful to the Community for all that opportunity represented.

Shortly before I became a bishop, I attended a reunion at Mirfield; we returned to the Leeds Hostel and were able to say the midday office in the chapel, which was now a lecture theatre. I recalled attending the daily Mass there as a nineteen- or twenty-year-old; I would occasionally look up at the priest at the altar and remind myself that the jewel of the priestly life was to offer Mass, and that, if all went well, I might be able to do that at twenty-five or twenty-six, fulfilling the greatest hope in my life. How many others could say that they would have fulfilled their ambition by the time they reached their mid-twenties? But first, I knew that I had to progress in my formation and to ensure that my 'ambition' was also what God wanted for me.

On Sunday nights we were allowed not to attend Evensong in the chapel but to visit other churches in and around Leeds. The Community of the Resurrection has always been Anglican Catholic, rather than Anglo-Papalist; however, a number of students would seek out the more 'advanced' churches, such as All Souls', Blackman Lane, where Father Hum was at one time 'under the ban' from the bishop. We used to enjoy going there for Vespers and Benediction. At least one notch down from All Souls was St. Aidan's Roundhay Park; I had been told that this was a fine church with mosaics, Italian marble, and a grand organ. Its worship included Solemn Evensong and Devotions to the Blessed Sacrament on Sunday evenings. A fellow student, Robert, and I boarded the bus in the centre of Leeds, but we had no idea where to get off, and asked two girls if they knew. To our surprise they said they were going to St. Aidan's, but did not know where to alight. Two or three times I looked at one of the girls, and she said, in quite a forthright way, but with a smile, 'Don't look at me - I don't know where to get off.' The two girls sat a few rows behind us in church. After the service we were too busy talking to the two Mirfield-trained priests on the staff to take any notice of the girls, and then we went off to do something we couldn't afford to do much of - to have a beer.

Next day at lunch, one of the students from the theology department said that he had heard I was on the bus to Roundhay and was spotted by Christine Jasper. I saw Christine on a couple of other occasions; one day, someone who was taking her to a dance and had to fall out, asked me to take his place, as he was sure that I would get on well with her. The students were also interested in her father, who was regularly in the church news - as this was the beginning of serious liturgical reform in the Church of England.

As well as being Chairman of the Liturgical Commission, Dr. Jasper was an historian, and, a few years previously, had written the life of Bishop Arthur Cayley Headlam of Gloucester. At that time, we were all awaiting the publication of his biography of George Bell, Bishop of Chichester (1929-58), one of the greatest bishops ever produced by the Church of England, who many expected to become the Archbishop of Canterbury in 1943, when William Temple died suddenly. Bishop Bell was a courageous church leader, who had helped Jews and others escape from Nazi Germany, and spoken out in the House of Lords against the indiscriminate bombing of German cities in the Second World War. He was a great ecumenist, theologian, and patron of the arts and a much-loved pastor. Christine had spent her previous summer holidays working on the index of this long-awaited biography. Dr. Jasper was always very humble and modest about his work and scholarship and would seldom initiate conversation about what he had achieved. As I became more involved with the family, I sensed that Bishop Bell had almost become part of the household; so the revelation fifty-seven years after his death that the Church had made an apology to one complainant on the grounds that the Bishop had abused her between sixty-five and seventy-five years ago seemed utterly unbelievable.

While the Church has been careful not to say that the Bishop is guilty, it has ruined his reputation. Originally, no information was given as to the process by which the Church had come to this conclusion, other than the statement that 'experts' had been involved. Such secrecy was hard to countenance in an age of 'transparency'. As a family, and in common with many others, we expressed our concern in the church press, and have continued to do so. In 2017, the Core Group Report was seriously criticised by Lord Carlile QC in his review into the Church's handling of the complaint.

Of course, it is right and proper that the Church investigates thoroughly every complaint made against every person and however famous and respected – and however ancient. Given, from the beginning, how shaky and questionable the allegation against Bishop Bell appeared to be, what has greatly concerned me is that the bishops of the Church of England, who, certainly in the past, had a fine reputation for standing against injustice and for being unafraid of making themselves unpopular, have expressed not one word of concern at the destruction of Bishop Bell - with the exception of the Bishop of Peterborough, in a speech in the House of Lords, and, more recently, the Bishop of Chester. A couple of retired bishops have voiced our concerns and given support to the George Bell Group, but our view carries little weight. Bishop Bell, a fellow bishop, stood for justice for a whole nation and many throughout the world. An allegation is made against him around sixty-five years later; he is tried by, frankly, what looks like a kangaroo court – with nobody to speak up for him, as Lord Carlile pointed out. Not a single bishop was prepared to query publicly what was being said and how it was being dealt with. The left-leaning newspapers, always eager to campaign on miscarriages of justice, have given scant support to those of us concerned at the traducing of Bell's reputation.

It has been left to *The Daily Telegraph*, *The Times* and *The Daily Mail* and *The Mail on Sunday* to write powerfully about the basic principles of justice being ignored by the Church. The Church is the Sacrament of the Kingdom, and becomes what she is meant to be in the celebration of the Eucharist - this keeps me going; it is the institutional church that gets so much wrong (as I know, also, from my own mistakes). I can therefore understand the anger and the real disappointment of the person who told me that 'the whole episode' of the church's handling of the Bishop Bell situation 'puts you off church-going'. My first concern as a bishop has always been for the survivor (even though I am aware of falling short some twenty-two years ago, when measured alongside today's strict and excellent standards); but until it can be proven beyond all reasonable doubt that Bishop Bell abused a child, I will continue to call upon George Bell within the Communion of Saints to pray with me and for me. Meanwhile I continue to treasure on my bookshelves Bishop Bell's copy of *The Oxford Dictionary of the Christian Church*, given to him on 7 October 1957.

Much has changed concerning Bishop Bell's reputation following further enquires, and the long awaited report of the Right Worshipful Timothy Briden, Vicar-General of Canterbury. What will not change, is the inadequate original investigation, and that George Bell, one of the 'saints' of the Church of England, who is commemorated every year (3rd Oct) in our liturgical calendar as bishop, ecumenist, and peacemaker (1958) should for the last four years have been cast into the wilderness by the Church he served with love and the greatest distinction.

Christine was two years ahead of me at University, so in my second year she was working for her Diploma in Education; she then went to live with her parents in Little Cloister, Westminster Abbey, and to take up her first teaching post, as head of Religious Education at Sydenham Girls High School. Meanwhile, I completed my degree in Religious Studies and History, and then went to the College of the Resurrection, Mirfield, commuting to Leeds for a further two years, as I was reading for the Postgraduate Diploma in Theology. We were married in Westminster Abbey on 17 July 1971, and our first house was Flat 1, The Lodge, at the entrance to the House, College and grounds of the Community of the Resurrection.

There were six married students at the time, and during my three years at The College (1970 – 1973) numbers were low – under twenty-six. Married students had a study in The College, and were fully integrated into the corporate life - wives were welcome at all meals. During Christine's two years at Mirfield she taught at Huddersfield Girls High School.

Ever since my first visit to the Community, in 1966, I

had always felt at ease at Mirfield - and I enjoyed my time at the College. While it was 'stricter' than at the

Our wedding reception, 17th July, 1971.

Hostel - we wore cassocks most of the time, for example - life for an ordinand in the 1970s was more relaxed than for earlier generations. So long as you were present at the daily services of Matins, Mass and Evensong, attended lectures and seminars, did your work, and participated in the common life, no-one breathed down your neck. The three-mile rule, about going into a pub, had been set aside, giving us access to the local pub, to the Labour Club and to the Working Men's Club (which faced one another across the road). A BBC reporter had referred to the College of the Resurrection as 'the commando course in the C of E', and maybe the life was more austere than in some of the other colleges - especially the Oxbridge ones (which with typical student exaggeration, we equated with gentlemen's clubs). Where the training at Mirfield excelled was in devotional formation – and, of course, we were blessed by living close to the Community. We had our Chapel in the Lower Church and joined the Community for daily Evensong, the Tuesday Conventual Mass, and for High Mass on Sundays and major festivals. Attendance at the midday Office and compline were optional for ordinands.

Holy Week at Mirfield was unforgettable. Most of the Community dispersed to assist with preaching and liturgy in parishes around the country, affording us the privilege of sitting in choir. During the first part of Holy Week there were lectures, which, in my first year, were delivered, in a helpfully accessible way, by Canon William Vanstone, one of the most brilliant of Anglican theologians. Paul Tillich, the German-American theologian, apparently described him as the best student to pass through his hands. Remarkably, he had turned aside from any of the academic appointments he had been offered, in order to be a parish priest, coming to us after many years of ministry on a housing estate on the outskirts of Rochdale. After the visiting lecturer left on Wednesday evening we would go into retreat - as best we could in view of the duties that fell to us over the Three Days (the Triduum). On Easter morning we would rise for the Easter Vigil at around 3.30am so that we were singing the Easter Gloria as the sun rose. At the end of this special time there would be a party, later on Easter Morning.

The theological formation was thorough. Ordinands who did not already possess a theology degree had to gain one at Leeds University in addition to their training at Mirfield. We were blessed at Leeds with a fine department of theology, led by Professor John Tinsley, who later became Bishop of Bristol. His 'Trinity' and 'Incarnation' course of lectures and seminars extended over one academic year, and his 'Atonement' course took place the following year, I have frequently returned to the substance of these courses over the years. A young theologian at the time, Dr Haddon Wilmer (some years later the Professor of Theology and Religious Studies at Leeds), also taught some doctrine, but was mainly a church historian; I had studied a lot of church history for my first degree and spent a considerable time with him. I am grateful to Haddon for 'extending' me, making me think, and helping me to acknowledge that I could set my sights higher.

The winds of change were blowing through the Church in the early seventies; they were becoming quite strong, and religious communities, theological colleges and seminaries were not sheltered from them. Speculative theology had considerable currency, and attention was focussed on the more radical theologians - especially those from Germany. I did my best to go along with this, and to come to a broad understanding of what it constituted, but my heart was with such traditional Anglican theologians as Michael Ramsey, Austin Farrer, Gregory Dix, William Temple, the Swedish Bishop Gustaf Aulen, and the Roman Catholic theologian Karl Rahner.

The college of the Resurrection, Mirfield, 1972. I am five from the right on the back row. My long standing close friends, Prebendary Alan Jones, back row first on the left and Fr. Denys Lloyd, CR, front row first on the right.

The Principal at Mirfield, Father William Wheeldon, a philosopher and a fine preacher, was intent on pushing us to think through our position, and not blindly to accept 'what the Church teaches'. He was plainly a bit unsettled himself, leaving the Community two or three years after I was ordained; initially he taught in a secondary school, but later came back to active ministry, as a parish priest. Shortly after he retired, I was presiding and preaching in a church in Derby where Fr. William had been the Vicar. While I was delighted to learn how well his ministry had been received, the description the parishioners gave of him was not quite how we would have described him in the 1970s – clearly, with marriage and being in a parish, he had mellowed somewhat over the years.

Fr. Benedict Green, the Vice-Principal, was an Old Etonian who seemed to have some knowledge of everything; he was a good New Testament scholar, and updated his father's commentary on St. Matthew while I was at Mirfield. I appreciated particularly his course on the doctrine of the Church and the sacraments - although at times he appeared to show some Lutheran sympathies. One student (Alan Jones), feeling put down by Fr. Benedict one day, exclaimed, 'But that's sheer Lutheranism Father', to which he replied, 'What's wrong with that?' Overall, Benedict represented a rock-solid presence, whatever was happening in college, and went on to be a much-loved Principal of Mirfield.

The one thing Fr. Benedict knew little about, was

driving a motor vehicle. One Friday evening we were at Leeds University and Benedict insisted on driving the mini-bus back to Mirfield. His clutch control was hopeless: we kangaroo-ed through the traffic, managed to go down a one-way street the wrong way, and were constantly in the wrong gear. During dinner that evening one student nipped out and put a note on his desk telling him to ring a Leeds number urgently. It was the number of the British School of Motoring.

Those of us who belonged to the theologically-conservative group within college always knew that the lecturer and tutor, Fr. Denys Lloyd, CR, was 'with us' – although, at that time, he would mark us down if we quarried our essays from traditional Roman Catholic sources. He went on to become Principal of the College and presided over it during a period of growth and strength, leaving the Community and the Church of England, in 1990, to test his vocation at Quarr Abbey. He is now the Roman Catholic Parish Priest at Sheringham and Cromer. I always had the greatest of confidence in Denys – to the extent that when he became a Roman Catholic, I questioned how I could stay, if he honestly felt that he could no longer remain in the Church of England. I weathered that particular storm - and many others from that direction over the years - and I am still here. While he remained at Mirfield, Denys joined Christine and me for a few days every summer, and continued to do so for some time after leaving the Church of England. Although Denys is thoroughly immersed in the Roman Church, he has not pulled down the curtain on previous

Anglican relationships, as some in his position have done. Christine and I have appreciated his friendship, rare insight, sense of humour, and so much more, over many years.

The general view in the Church of England while I was training, and certainly at Mirfield, was that theological college was a place of spiritual and theological formation and that the development of the pastoral side was left for the deacon's year and the remainder of the title ministry. One sign that was beginning to change in my time, was the presence on staff of Fr. David Jackson, who was not of the Community, although he had been a Mirfield ordinand. Before taking up his post, Fr David had been a parish priest in the Diocese of Southwark - so his appointment clearly signalled a greater focus on pastoral training. Weekly hospital visits took place with a month-long hospital course in the long vacation; there were also parish attachments, school teaching weeks, and prison visiting opportunities.

I made good friends at Mirfield, and Christine and I have kept up with some of them; practically everybody who was at the College during my three years has continued to serve in the priesthood, which, given the turbulent times and huge changes in both Church and society, must indicate that the training given was solid enough to carry us through some difficult times.

One significant issue that was beginning to surface in my time at Mirfield, was the question of the ordination of women. It was spoken about, but no one seriously expected it to roll far down the track. Mrs Wickham (the wife of the Bishop of Middleton) and Mrs Charles (the wife of Canon Sebastian Charles) came to address the Common Room on the subject, and I recall that their arguments were rather emotive. There were some students who were mildly sympathetic - but Geoffrey Kirk and James Bell, and some other sharp minded people, were not at all sympathetic. Mrs Wickham said to Mrs Charles, 'We're clearly not going to get anywhere here, we might as well go.' I recall the Principal trying to be quite diplomatic; he talked about a pilot scheme that, if it did not work, involved sending the women off to be cathedral canons. This was in 1972 - if anyone had told me that this question would take centre stage and remain there throughout my active ministry, I would never have believed them. In the event, from that time onwards there were to be few days when this issue did not occupy some of my thinking time.

I have always been grateful for my training at Mirfield. I later became a Priest Companion of the Fraternity of the Resurrection and went there for my annual retreat many times – and for my pre-Consecration Retreat, During my time in Blackburn my confessor was at Mirfield. I therefore regularly visited the House, and took the College Ash Wednesday Retreat in the first year that women were invited to train there. Later on, at my last Bishop's Staff Meeting in Blackburn, I took the whole staff to Mirfield, and, after lunch, we were taken round the restored Community Church.

The modern College is described in these terms, 'The College of the Resurrection has changed greatly over the years, keeping pace with the changing world of ministerial formation, and is now part of a widespread training network, covering Yorkshire and further afield. It remains, however, a theological college like no other, giving students direct engagement with the monastic tradition, centred in God and prayer' (*A Brief History: The Community of The Resurrection*, Mirfield Publications, 2013). I praise God that while methods have changed, the aim and ethos at the College of the Resurrection have remained constant.

3   GETTING GOING – THE BLACK COUNTRY, ST. CHAD'S, COSELEY

In June 1973 we left for St. Chad's Coseley, in the Diocese of Lichfield, which had been my home diocese since 1961. Fr. Arthur Williams was my first training incumbent, an old student of the College, of whom the Principal and other Brethren of the Community spoke highly. I was ordained deacon in Lichfield Cathedral on 1 July. Although I had a degree and a Postgraduate Diploma and had passed the General Ordination Examination, we all had to write two long essays for the Bishop before we could be ordained. It was difficult to know what the purpose of this was, but the Principal informed me it was to see who would read the Gospel at the Ordination – and, to my huge surprise, the Director of Ordinands told me that I had been chosen. In consequence I was the last to be ordained by the bishop, and immediately after laying hands on me, he handed the Book of the Gospels to me to proclaim the Good News of Jesus Christ.

I took part in Evensong that night in the Parish Church and there was a parish get together afterwards. Both Christine and I immediately warmed to the congregation. After the Ordination, the bishop expected the newly-ordained deacon, his wife and parents, to join him for a buffet lunch at Bishop's House. I asked in advance whether I could bring my parents-in-law as well - given my father-in-law's position, the bishop was delighted to agree. Bishop Stretton Reeve had a reputation for knowing all his clergy by name - by surname, of course - and for circulating at gatherings. Accordingly, I was rather surprised that he spent so much time with my father-in-law - I only learnt the reason on the following Wednesday.

On that day my father attended the funeral of the Lord Lieutenant at St. Mary's Stafford, and, as he was shaking the bishop's hand after the service, he mentioned that he had ordained me the previous Sunday. When the bishop heard of the connection, he took my father to one side and asked him to use his powers of persuasion to encourage me to accompany my incumbent to Holy Trinity Wordsley, ten miles from St. Chad's, when he moved there a few months later. The penny dropped about the long conversation on the Sunday, and I have always been grateful to my father-in-law for not saying anything about his conversation with the bishop on the day of my ordination.

The bishop rang up on the Thursday and asked me to come over to Lichfield; he told me that he was moving Fr. Williams and I should go with him. I did not want to move to Wordsley, which, at that time, had a 'middle of the road' tradition, with no Reservation of the Blessed Sacrament - the priest celebrating the Eucharist in 'a shirt' (surplice and stole). It was nowhere near as *gritty* as St. Chad's. As at Mirfield, I had already come to feel that Coseley was absolutely right for me. Bishop Reeve was a very big man, and when he spoke it was 'Thus saith the Lord'. When I reminded him that the previous curate had left in a hurry, 'under a cloud', and it would be difficult for this parish to see both its vicar and new curate leave together, he was more sympathetic. However, the objection which seemed to 'clinch' it, was when I told him that Christine was Head of Religious Education at Dudley Girls' High School, that this was a real vocation for her, and, as she could not drive, it would take three buses to get from Wordsley to Dudley. I said the journey was practically impossible, and she would have to resign, and have no job. The bishop accepted that, and said I could remain at St Chad's. We were relieved.

St. Chad's enjoyed 'full Catholic privileges', as we used to say; the genius of Father Williams was that, without diluting the tradition, he had made it a warm parish community, with the Mass at the heart of its life and every conceivable other activity. It was a true Parish Family; we were an 'outreaching' Church – and there was compulsory visiting for the clergy every afternoon from 2.00 to 5.00 and again in the evening (if there were no activities to attend). There was an underlying conviction that 'a priest in the home means people in church'. It is easy to dismiss this approach, but it has some validity. We became known in pubs and clubs, had our own church school - but we also went into other schools and were welcomed there. If I had my time over again, I would spend more of it in schools, making sure I was better equipped for this special ministry. We are missing out on an important pastoral and mission opportunity by not maximising our involvement in schools.

If we knew of people from the parish in hospital, we

would go and visit them, whether they came to church or not. Indeed, when I went into the local hospitals, I would always ask to see the list of patients so I could visit them, as well as our own congregation. Imparting such information to a priest - or to anyone - today is illegal. But for us, such pastoral contacts were a great asset; the aim was not just to fill pews, although some of those we visited did subsequently come to Church. Recently I had a letter from one person whom I had visited while recovering from major surgery, who subsequently became a key member of the congregation for nearly forty-five years.

In those days we had our Missions and Teaching Weeks; but we focused primarily on pastoral openings and on the mission opportunities that came our way through careful preparation for the occasional offices. With funerals, for instance, there were follow-up visits and a memorial service combined with Evensong on the following Sunday. We took care to prepare couples for marriage, and to get to know them and to attend their receptions afterwards. Some couples would wait until the service was over, and only if they felt sure you were a fully paid-up member of the human race would they invite you to the reception – often at the signing of the Register. I soon learnt that if you were there at the time of the speeches, you would usually be asked to speak. It is good to see the Church taking the occasional offices more seriously. I was delighted in Blackburn when we were chosen to be one of the pilot dioceses for the Wedding Project.

What I learnt at St. Chad's was to be a community priest, meeting people 'where they were' and trying to be gentle with them. We cannot force, drag or scold people into the Kingdom; we can only love them into the Kingdom - and much of that pastoral understanding I acquired from Father Williams. He left me for Wordsley on All Saints' Day, but in the few months I was with him he taught me so much, and I am forever indebted to him.

There was a daily Mass at St. Chad's, but numbers were not exceptional, largely because nearly everybody went out to work; but if you were a member of St. Chad's you came on Sundays, so numbers did not fluctuate much at the major festivals. If someone was not present, we would assume sickness was the reason for it, and make an enquiry. People would be very disappointed if they were unwell and you did not contact them.

I know it is easy to idealise the past and, of course, it was a different age then, and the Church was still seen to be an important player in the community, but everything seemed to hum in that parish. During my training I had heard that the Church was losing ground, and that we needed to change dramatically, so it was such an encouragement to go to a parish that worked. There was a good number of young people, men and women. There was a keen and well-supported branch of the Church of England Men's Society, which had a monthly Mass and corporate communion, a social evening, a working party evening, 'Big Steak' nights out – and there was always beer after meetings.

It was something of a culture shock when we arrived at St. Chad's. Many of the folk lived in the kitchen, the chip pan was usually on, and 'Tea' was the main meal of the day. In my first few weeks there, when Christine was completing her teaching contract in Huddersfield, I was looked after by the parish. I always had a good lunch out, and was then invited to Tea at 5.00 pm - a roast beef meal, only three hours after I had finished lunch. The meal had to be at 5.00 because the men folk returned at that time and would want their meal before going out - frequently to church events.

In the deanery there were twelve curates, all of us stipendiary. I think there are no more than two or three now, and not all 'full-time'. I was fortunate to have Alan Jones as my neighbour; he had been with me at the College of the Resurrection and has remained one of my very closest friends. One of the finest Black Country priests, Alan became a Prebendary of Lichfield Cathedral in 2011, and I was privileged to be there for his installation. He died very suddenly in early 2018, having just taken the retirement post of Interim Priest at Coven outside Wolverhampton. I was honoured to be the Principal Celebrant at his Funeral Mass, concelebrating with forty-six priests of The Society of SS. Wilfrid and Hilda. I miss him very much - especially his lengthy phone calls.

Alan came from Bilston, had been a Roman Catholic and was destined for the seminary; but he read Michael Ramsey's book, 'The Gospel and the Catholic Church' (first published in 1936 and slightly revised in

1955), and began to see the Church of England for what it is - a branch of the Catholic Church. As an Anglican, he soon found his way to Prebendary Philip Husbands, Rector of St. James' Wednesbury, who did all things Roman; but when the Series 2 Church of England Eucharistic Rite came, he immediately started using it and installed a nave altar. The bishop then began to view him differently, and used him more in the diocese. Philip Husbands served on the General Synod for many years, was sharp, intelligent, wise and a fine parish priest; he knew and understood his people, had a keen wit, and a view on most things. He was a priest to whom young Catholic clergy could always turn for excellent advice, and it was not always what we wanted to hear.

Alan and I saw things very much in the same light, although, without having my Anglican background, he found it less easy to accommodate those of a more liberal persuasion and was clear and firm on ecumenical relations. While the modern Ecumenical Movement can be seen to have had its beginnings with the 1910 Edinburgh Conference and the coming into being of the World Council of Churches in 1948, the years following the Second Vatican Council (which closed in 1965) saw the Roman Catholic Church demonstrating a real commitment to the work of unity. The 1970s were therefore times of exciting ecumenical developments. There had been setbacks even during these heady years: looking back, it seems to me that the failures came about largely because the ecumenical schemes were being imposed by Church leaders and theologians and with little serious engagement with congregations. They were 'top down' schemes.

One 'headline scheme' during these years was the Anglican-Methodist Unity Scheme, which was unsuccessful in 1969, and again in 1972. As a student, I took some interest in this issue, and, at the time, I would have supported the Scheme, because I thought the proposed Service of Reconciliation of Ministries was sound, and appeared to be the most satisfactory attempt to reunite an episcopal Church with a non-episcopal one. It was being supported by Archbishop Ramsey, Dr. Eric Kemp, then Dean of Worcester, Dr. Robert Mortimer, Bishop of Exeter, Prebendary Philip Husbands, and most of the Community of the Resurrection. At the end of the 1970s another attempt at wider unity was made with the Covenanting for Unity proposals between the Church of England, the Baptist Union, the Methodist Church, the Moravian Church and the United Reformed Church, which simply invited us all to accept one another as true Churches within the One Church of Christ and to recognise and accept one another's ministry and Sacraments without any form of reconciliation. This made it much more difficult for very many of us to accept than the earlier Anglican-Methodist Scheme - in my view it was unsatisfactory.

Perhaps I was being too simplistic, but I recall standing up at the Deanery Synod and saying that what was proposed in 'covenanting for unity' was as absurd as putting a notice on the church notice-board informing everyone that unless they wrote in they would all be considered to be confirmed. The proposals were not passed by the General Synod, and, over the last two decades, more energy has been put into growing together at the level of individual parishes, congregations, groups and deaneries, and church leaders working together in common witness. I think it was Cardinal Cormac Murphy O'Connor who said that doctrinal agreement between the churches is important, but so is sharing a bowl of pasta and perhaps a glass of wine.

The later Anglican-Methodist Covenant of 2003 represented a wiser way forward, and, during my time in Blackburn, I much enjoyed working with Stephen Poxon, the Chair of the Northwest Lancashire District. We agreed to take the Covenant a stage further in certain situations by offering clergy and ministers the opportunity of sacramental ministry in each other's churches. When the Methodist Chairs met the House of Bishops at Lambeth Palace in 2006, Stephen and I appeared to be somewhat 'ahead of the game'. Much time and energy was put into ecumenism in Lancashire, and there was real commitment from all the leaders to our gatherings and activities - perhaps especially from Archbishop Patrick of Liverpool, whose archdiocese covered three Churches Together areas, and who was often to be seen in all three.

Strangely, the Coseley and neighbouring parishes were not deterred by the failed attempts to bring about organic unity in 1972. For the most part we accepted the 1952 Lund Principle, which had stated that at every level of its life we be urged 'to act together and in concert with other churches of Jesus Christ in all matters except those in which deep differences of conviction or church order compel us to act separately'. I believe we attempted - to a varying extent - to do just that, enjoying one another's company, and holding an impressive number of events during the Week of Prayer for Christian Unity, including a dance event in the canteen of a local steel works. Each summer we chartered a train to a cathedral city, and attended one another's churches. Anglican churches with social clubs and bars enrolled some members from other churches, including the occasional Free Church Minister.

I was blessed with the opportunity of experiencing at close quarters the changing climate in the Roman Catholic Church when, six months after my ordination to the priesthood, I went to Rome (for the first time) with David Jasper, my brother-in-law, who was completing his ordination training at St. Stephen's House, Oxford. David and the Vice-Rector of the English College in Rome were engaged in a joint project, and I accompanied him on Boxing Day 1974 for a six-day stay at the English College. (The College provides a highly specialised formation for selected seminarians from England.) As a recently ordained priest, I found the College considerably more relaxed than I expected (and in some respects more so than Mirfield). There appeared to be an openness that one did not find in Anglo-Catholic circles.

Two ordinands from Anglican colleges had just completed an exchange, one from the Anglo-Catholic college, St. Stephen's House, Oxford, and one from St. John's College, Nottingham, a more charismatic and evangelical college. I was astonished to find that a number of the seminarians found the student from St. John's College more in tune with them; when I enquired why, they said, 'The Catholic Church is changing; we have gone back to the Bible.' Mgr Murphy O'Connor was the Rector - I thought he struck a good balance in implementing change without losing the received wisdom of the past.

The day after our arrival, I spoke to the Vice-Rector about the Eucharist; he seemed somewhat apologetic that I could not concelebrate with them, saying that the College had given an undertaking to the bishops that this would not happen. It was their hope that I would say Mass at the Venerable Bede altar, using their vessels. When I enquired if any Anglican priests had ever celebrated there, he said, 'only one - Archbishop Michael Ramsey, when he made his historic visit to Pope Paul VI eight years previously'. I could not believe it. That visit of the Archbishop to the Pope had established the Anglican-Roman Catholic International Commission (ARCIC); their task was 'to engage in a serious dialogue which, founded on the Gospels and on the ancient traditions, may lead to that unity in truth, for which Christ prayed.' The College and Rome seemed abuzz, expecting that there would be a Unity Scheme in due course. Indeed, the Commission worked quite swiftly and, by 1981, had published three 'Agreed Statements' - on the Eucharist, Ordained Ministry, and Authority in the Church.

Not everyone in Rome in 1974 was enthusiastic or optimistic about Canterbury and Rome becoming much closer. I was therefore very grateful to sit next to a Monsignor from one of the dicasteries at the celebratory Lunch on the College Foundation Day, the Feast of St. Thomas à Becket. He was warm and courteous, but early in the conversation made it clear that, in spite of there being a good head of steam, very substantial hurdles remained to be overcome. There was no prospect of a uniat or other scheme coming about in the near future. Over the years I have never forgotten those words.

My visit to Rome that Christmas week, those whom I met, and everything I heard and saw, convinced me that the principal focus for unity for the Church of England and the Anglican Communion, should be upon the Great Church of the West, and the work of ARCIC. I most certainly could not have believed that the next time I went to Rome, forty-two years later, while ARCIC was still a work in progress, all talk of 'unity in the foreseeable future' had been abandoned. Provision had been made for an Anglican Ordinariate allowing bishops, priests and congregations to come into full communion with the Roman Catholic Church and to retain some of their Anglican worship and traditions. While this showed signs of great understanding for the predicament faced by Catholic Anglicans, following the Ordination of Women to the priesthood, and also great generosity from the Pope, it is not what was envisaged by ARCIC.

A year after my ordination as deacon I had returned with Alan Jones (serving in the neighbouring parish) and all my contemporaries for Deacons' Week. On Sunday 29 June I was ordained Priest by the Lord Bishop in Lichfield Cathedral using the 1662 Rite. There was a distinctive local custom that the bishop would suspend the laying on of hands half-way through, and then resume with the other half of the semi-circle following the singing of a hymn. I was the first in the semi-circle to be ordained after the break. On the coach to the Cathedral one of the candidates disclosed that he had dreamt the night before, that the Bishop had collapsed after he had ordained the first twelve in the semicircle. I admit I did recall his dream during the service - but all was well. I was especially delighted that day to have my old headmaster from Normandale School in Bexhill present, and he remained for my first Mass that evening in St. Chad's Church.

Although concelebration of the Eucharist was catching on in the Church of England, at St. Chad's we still had the High Mass, though westward facing; the deacon was Fr. Denys Lloyd, CR, a tutor from the College of the Resurrection, who had been to St. Chad's to celebrate all the Christmas Masses during the vacancy. The sub-deacon was Fr. Derek Hanscombe, the new vicar, and my father-in-law, Dr. Ronald Jasper, by then Archdeacon of Westminster, preached. I asked him not to speak at all about me – in the event he preached a powerful sermon on the exemplary character of the ministry of the greatly-revered slum priest, Father Wainwright of St. Peter's London Docks. Father Leslie Warrington, whom I had first encountered many years before, at St. James' Salt, led the Bidding Prayers. The next day I celebrated a Requiem Mass for my departed relatives, and my third Mass was of Our Lady.

I was grateful to my confessor and director at the time, Father John Bigby at Holy Trinity Ettingshall, Wolverhampton, for teaching me to hear confessions; and I still look back on Kenneth Ross' book, *Hearing Confessions,* as one of the most helpful aids. There was a handful of regular penitents in the parish; but during my visits to hospitals and homes, I soon discovered that many more wanted to 'sacramentalise' our pastoral conversations. Whether or not confessions are regularly heard in a parish, priests may be called upon at any time to hear a confession and give absolution - they must be trained to do so, and be ready at all times to celebrate the Sacrament of Reconciliation.

The vacancy at St. Chad's catapulted me into a very responsible role, just four months after ordination - and the interregnum lasted four months. The new parish priest, Father Derek Hanscombe, had been trained at Chichester, an Anglo-Catholic college, and came to us from his post as the diocesan youth chaplain. Derek and his wife, Susan, were kind and supportive - but I of course 'knew it all' by that time, as I had been 'running' this big parish for four months. Frankly, I was arrogant. Derek had a different approach, and, in the event, I learnt much from him. If I had been more humble, I would have learnt a lot more. I shall always be grateful to Derek for giving me a fairly free hand to develop and grow, even when it was not always in the way he would have chosen - and he was always there whenever I made a mess of things and needed him. Derek could see that the world was changing and that the Church needed to speak to and identify with this emerging society. He stayed at the parish for four years, bringing St. Chad's into a new era, and paving the way for his successor, Fr. Melvyn Smith, who had known the parish for a number of years.

Derek's next post was as USPG (United Society for the Propagation of the Gospel) Training Officer, subsequently undertaking a number of innovative projects. His untimely death, in 1996, deprived the Church of a radical voice - in tune with young people - which the Church needed to hear and to be challenged by. I have enjoyed keeping in touch with Susan and their eldest son, Stephen, whom I helped to prepare for confirmation and who was subsequently ordained priest in Ripon and Leeds Diocese in 2016.

Father Williams, my very first vicar at St. Chad's Coseley, who had been at Holy Cross Bilbrook before coming to St. Chad's, always said what a wonderful curate-in-charge post Holy Cross was - the Anglo-Catholic curate's dream second curacy. Fr. Christopher Hill from a neighbouring catholic parish in the Black Country had gone to Holy Cross, but quite swiftly moved to Lambeth to be one of the two Archbishops' Counsellors on Foreign Relations, and Anglican Secretary to the Anglican Roman Catholic International Commission. (Christopher was later to became Bishop of Guildford just after I became Bishop of Blackburn.) My friend, Fr. Keith Wassall, from an adjacent parish, went to replace Christopher, so I thought I would not, in the future, have the chance to go to Holy Cross. Keith was a fine priest but a plain-spoken one, and would always have 'his say' – whoever he was speaking to. The Vicar of Codsall, in whose parish Bilbrook was situated, was from the 'old school' and did not like anyone rocking the boat - so he and Keith were on a collision course. The upshot was that after just six months or so, Keith decided to take a post in the Hanley Team Ministry with Ray Funnell (who later became Dean of York), and Bilbrook was vacant again. Father Williams put my name forward.

When I met the Vicar, Prebendary Gilbert Smith, and his Standing Committee, I realised that I would be able to get along with him, but that I would need to hone my diplomatic skills to do so. Bilbrook was a very large, separate area in the parish with a high proportion of social housing. By contrast, the parish church was relatively 'up-market' with a Parish Communion tradition – as Bilbrook was a 'five-star, modern catholicism' church, and rather different in character, Prebendary Smith was generally content to leave the priest there to 'get on with it'. We were sad to be leaving St. Chad's after two wonderful years, but I thanked God for my new challenge, which was everything I could have wanted.

4. 'DROP IT OLD BOY' – THE BILBROOK YEARS

As I was technically curate-in-charge of Holy Cross and curate of Codsall there was no need for a special service in the parish with the Bishop to launch my ministry. I went over to Lichfield some months later to be licensed in the Bishop's Chapel by the new Bishop, Kenneth Skelton. Instead, on 2 July, we had a concelebrated Eucharist with my new congregation; many came from St. Chad's and the Vicar of Codsall preached.

Two weeks later, I took a coach party up to Mirfield for Commemoration Day, which was always a great jamboree. This presented me with a great opportunity to 'work the coach,' getting to know my new congregation. My first three parishes all loved coach outings - in those days it was possible to have a beer on the coach without the fear of some passengers drinking to excess and slashing the seats. The coach was always late back because it was not considered 'a day out' unless we stopped for fish and chips on the way home.

The sacristy attached the priest's house to the church, which was very convenient – although, occasionally, people would just appear in the kitchen. The bus stop was right outside the house and from the top of the bus the passengers could just about see into our bedroom - there was no point in retiring to bed before 11.10 pm when the last bus arrived. The garden was used as a litter bin for chip papers. Nevertheless, it was a real blessing to live in the centre of the community, opposite the shops and with the school a few doors along. 'The Woodman' public house was next door to the Church Hall.

As at St. Chad's, I saw myself as a community priest; the daily routine was very similar, and the activities and concerns into which I was drawn were practically the same - only now I had much more responsibility. I could not cut my teeth in a better place; at this time the Church was beginning to look at new means of reaching out to people. With a very supportive congregation behind me I could make mistakes, and see them as a learning experience, without anyone saying, 'told you so'.

There was indeed a good congregation, and it grew - so much so that we needed more chairs in the rear part of the building. We saw some advertised cheaply in a church in Crawley, some two hundred-and-fifty miles away. I went to inspect them with my friend Fr. Alan Jones. When I reported this to the Parochial Church Council (PCC) at Codsall, I reminded them how poor we were at Holy Cross and that we could not afford to pay for the transportation of the chairs, and one of the members sent a lorry from his firm in Wolverhampton to collect them. Everything had to be done on the cheap (and often for free) in the West Midlands churches in which I worked. On countless occasions people outside the church would offer to do something free of charge because of the bank of goodwill that the church had established.

The people took their worship seriously. Holy Cross, again, was a church where if someone was not present on Sunday, it could safely be assumed that they were ill. Attendance at daily Mass was encouraging, and a few lay people also attended daily Matins and Evensong, and there were a few regular penitents. Holy Week - especially The Great Three Days - was a powerful experience. The congregation heeded the teaching that there is a thread that runs through the whole week, especially the sacred three days. People accepted that attendance just on Palm Sunday and on Easter Day would not enable them to journey with the Lord in His saving passion and death and rising from the dead.

The congregation would back all of the church's activities: not just worship, but also pastoral projects, teaching, working parties and social events. The church was full of devotion and enthusiasm, and needed a greater degree of independence in order to move forward. We were not even supposed to have social events, because the whole parish was signed up to a version of Christian Stewardship which bound its members to give sacrificially and in return solicited no further contributions - thereby prohibiting fund-raising events, including dances. I frequently challenged the Vicar about this - and (although we liked one other) he would simply raise his hand and say, 'drop it old boy'. I felt that I had no choice but to determine, with the Bilbrook Church Committee, that we should press on with our programme of renewal and greater independence - albeit in as discreet a way as possible.

On one occasion I recall asking the Vicar if we could have the Bishop to visit, to encourage the congregation - I was told that the Bishop always visits the Parish Church, not Holy Cross. I argued that this was the problem, that no Bishop had ever been to Bilbrook. Again, I was told, 'drop it old boy!'

The new Bishop of Stafford, John Waine (who left the diocese far too early, to become Bishop of Edmundsbury and Ipswich, and subsequently Bishop of Chelmsford) had special oversight of junior clergy; when I told him what was going on at Bilbrook, he said that he would come and see it all for himself, and that was the end of the matter. He visited us for Holy Cross Day, our feast of title (September 14). So powerful was that night that it effectively constituted a mini-mission. Gilbert, the Vicar, decided to attend, to concelebrate and to join the party in the hall afterwards. The issue of having bishops at 'the daughter church' seemed to have been forgotten; the following year we had Bishop John Daly (former Bishop of Korea) who had the Holy Cross Mission Sisters in his diocese. Six months before I left Holy Cross parish, the diocesan bishop himself visited us.

I realised at Bilbrook that I could not move forward with our agenda by the use of argument and muscle alone. Accordingly I fulfilled my duties at the mother church, St. Nicholas' Codsall, as conscientiously as I could, and always tried to support the Vicar. This was especially the case when he sought my support in his capacity as Rural Dean at clergy chapter meetings, which some took as an opportunity to wind him up. I was usually able to make Gilbert laugh, and had no difficulty in relating to the more 'up-market' people whom he was so anxious not to upset.

The bishop and the archdeacon took seriously our call for Bilbrook to have its own full-time resident priest – to be known as 'District Minister' initially - and I was hoping to be the first post-holder, and to get free of Gilbert, my old friend (and he really was that). However, there was to be a condition attached. My father-in-law had become Dean of York since our move to Bilbrook; we were having a few days off in York, and went for an afternoon to Whitby. On the cliffs there we saw the Bishop of Stafford; he greeted us and told me that I should move to St. Peter's Upper Gornal, where I would train a curate and be a hospital chaplain and have a much bigger job. When I expressed my wish to stay at Bilbrook and become the first 'Vicar,' he said that he did not believe in priests building their own empires. The work had been done and someone else should be the first priest under the new scheme. That certainly blew a relaxing few days away.

The Catholic Faith just seemed natural at Holy Cross. There had been a succession of young, dynamic, Catholic clergy, and the more recent priests had tended to be of the Roman 'post-conciliar' variety. I certainly tried to keep things within bounds, and there was never much discussion about what was done. It was accepted as a 'given', and the young people thought what went on there was normal Church of England practice, and when we went to other services in the deanery 'further down the candle,' I had to explain that the Church of England is a broad tent, but that we had 'got it right'!

The whole congregation, including our young people, loved the annual weekend pilgrimage to the Shrine of Our Lady of Walsingham, in spite of the more primitive accommodation in those days; it was a good way of keeping the young with us, sustaining a good choir and youth group in the process. I am delighted that in all the parishes in which I worked I have been able to lead pilgrimages to the Shrine. It is a powerful witness to the Incarnation - a place where faith grows, lives are changed, and people brought to a deeper sacramental life. Many are introduced to new devotions, while meeting others for whom the Catholic Life lived in the Church of England is simply the normal way. The pilgrimage has always been a fun weekend and we invariably returned with stories to share.

Walsingham is an important ecumenical centre, and it was clear that many Christians saw Our Lord's Mother not as a stumbling block to unity, but as a significant path to further unity. Indeed, if we are to have the Christian Faith in its fullness we cannot fail to embrace Our Lady's part in the story of our salvation. Interestingly she is rarely represented by herself, but is usually holding her Son up or pointing to Him, and devotion can only increase when we come to see this as her role.

At this time in my life, I came into contact with the Ecumenical Society of the Blessed Virgin Mary, which had been founded in 1967 to advance the study of the place of the Blessed Virgin in the Church under Christ and to promote ecumenical devotion. The Society produced interesting, and sometimes very learned, papers and also had a more popular edge, so I became a member and encouraged others at Holy Cross to join me. When a new branch opened in Wolverhampton in 1976, the speakers were Dr. Langton-Fox, the Roman Catholic Bishop of Menevia, John Waine, Bishop of Stafford and Joe Cleary, Roman Catholic Auxiliary Bishop in Birmingham Archdiocese, and the Revd. Nigel Gilson, Chairman of the Shrewsbury Methodist District. It was an amazing inaugural meeting, with a packed church - Bishop Langton-Fox, the principal speaker who had recently experienced a 'charismatic conversion', had us all spell bound. An enthusiastic branch was born, and I was elected to the executive and served as treasurer.

At first, I feared that the Ecumenical Society would attract just Roman Catholics and High Church Anglicans, but in the event it did extend its reach to other sections of the Church of England, and there was keen involvement from the Free Churches. Indeed, the best book I have read on the rosary was written by the Methodist Minister, J. Neville Ward, *Five for Sorrow, Ten for Joy* (published in 1971). Some former parishioners may well recall the quotations from it that I used in my sermons. In 1982, shortly after I moved to East Sussex, I formed the East Sussex Branch of the

Ecumenical Society of the B.V.M. with Canon Derek Allen (the former Principal of St. Stephen's House.) While I am still a member of the Society, in the last two decades my attendance has been very infrequent. I was delighted when those attending the International Conference of the Society in Lancashire in 2010 came to Blackburn Cathedral and I was able to preside and preach at the main Eucharist. At the Conference Dinner, Bishop Ambrose Griffiths OSB who was chairing the conference suggested that I should speak, the scheduled speaker having failed to arrive - this only gave me the main course and the pudding to prepare. It is pleasing to see that branches of the Society are still being formed or re-formed, and that conferences still held. My experience has shown me that in turning to sacred scripture and ancient shared traditions concerning the Mother of God incarnate, our joint understanding of and devotion to Mary in the communion of saints grows, and in doing so leads us to deeper unity.

For most of our fairly short time at Bilbrook, Christine continued to teach at Dudley Girls' High School - but just as we were about to leave the parish, our lives changed, with the arrival of Claire, who was born on 4 January 1978. Our final Mass at Holy Cross was on 2 February, when, a little over two-and-a-half very happy years in my first charge, we went back to the Black Country with Claire - to live at the top of the same road in which we had lived when I was curate at St. Chad's.

5   BACK TO THE BLACK COUNTRY, ST. PETER'S UPPER GORNAL

We moved into a ten-year-old vicarage, which looked as if it belonged on the side of a mountain in Switzerland. It was hardly the most appropriate accommodation for the priest, situated immediately behind 'The White City', where all the houses were grey, and owned by the local authority - hardly any of them became owner-occupied when the incoming Conservative administration, eighteen months later, made it possible for council tenants to purchase their rented accommodation. The vicarage was never really warm, and we put this down to its being open-plan; after we left, the new boiler engineers said the size of the pump was far too small for the system and the central heating radiators were sparingly distributed, so baby Claire's room could have been warmer.

The Institution and Induction, with Bishop John Waine of Stafford, took place on a freezingly cold night, but the clergy - especially the diocesan Federation of Catholic Priests - and many friends, turned up in full force. Whether any of the visitors came out of curiosity to see the new Licensing and Institution Service being used for the first time in the diocese, I do not know. (I did not rate it very highly.)

The Church of England, of course, must have a service which lasts at least an hour, and I had been told that we were not allowed to have the Institution with the Eucharist. I had shown the new service to my father-in-law, who was still Chairman of the General Synod Liturgical Commission, and so I was delighted when, over an early supper before the Institution, he said to the Bishop that he could not understand why in this service we carried up bread, wine and water and a chalice and paten, and then did not have a Eucharist. I did enjoy getting in before the Bishop could respond with 'but we're not allowed to have one in this diocese.' I promised Bishop John, while he was vesting for the service, that I did not put my father-in-law up to making that observation.

Despite all the arguments of divisiveness, and the fear of the Church of England being seen to be sectarian, I fail to understand to this day why, on the occasion of a priest being instituted to a ministry of word and sacrament by the principal minister of word and sacrament in the diocese, the service can only be one of the word. Thankfully, not every diocese took this view, although I still found, twenty-five years later, some on the Bishop's Staff in Blackburn who supported it - but I made provision there for the Institution or Licensing to be within the Eucharist.

I was fortunate to inherit Fr. Colin Preece, who was a very capable curate, well able to show me the ropes in this large and densely-populated parish, with a number of very real social issues. There was also a hospital chaplaincy to work. Colin was ready for his first responsibility, leaving me after four months. We decided to replace the not very adequate curate's house - in those days the parish had to find the money to house a curate, rather than the diocese.

St. Peter's clergy had been of Tractarian sympathy from an early stage, although a distinctively Catholic tradition had only been established in the last fifteen to twenty years. The daily Mass, and Reservation of the Blessed Sacrament and other features, were well accepted, and not contentious. Incense, however, was introduced later on, and even then restricted to use at festivals celebrated during the week. The parish did not want to be 'too High' partly because at the neighbouring church, St. James' Lower Gornal, they had incense every Sunday and a reputation for being 'very High'.

To begin with some were a little suspicious of me because of my first two appointments. While I have always been a community priest, and never felt it right to impose an inappropriate style of worship on a congregation, I have never pretended to be anything other than a Catholic Anglican. It also needs to be remembered that this was the time of liturgical renewal, and some saw the new services as pushing the church 'up the candle'. While we were at St. Peter's, *The Alternative Service Book* (1980) was published; my father-in-law had been the chief architect of it, and piloted it through the General Synod (what a task for him, but he always said he never lost any sleep over it). The congregation was delighted to receive signed copies of the new book from him.

Although there was a good congregation and some fine lay leadership - particularly with confirmation candidates and young people - the church was ripe for further development and growth. There was also an urgent need to maximise our income - but the PCC had set its face against Christian Stewardship some years before, and would not budge. Thankfully, within eighteen months, we were to have a very successful campaign, which did not only produce a greatly increased income, but also a generous response of 'time and talents'. We had to be careful whom we sent on stewardship visits - one or two members of the congregation picked up the wrong end of the stick, and thought it involved appointing 'shop stewards' from their number. Nevertheless, I firmly believe the campaign reaped a rich harvest, because we treated it as a mission to the church to facilitate a wider mission to the parish, ensuring sustained growth in the congregation.

In those opening months we had to raise money urgently for the church hall because its flat roof was leaking badly. The church was in the centre of the community, opposite the shops, and *The Shakespeare* public house – always known as 'The Shack' - where there was the odd fight and from which 'flying pickets' would be picked up during industrial disputes. Indeed, within four hundred yards of the church there were six drinking establishments, including the Gornal and Sedgley Labour Club, which was very much the heart of the community. If I was there on a Friday night they would always offer me the microphone and invite me to say a few words; some of the ordination candidates who were on placement from the College of the Resurrection Mirfield were also made to do a stint in there, and to answer questions (one of them was not pleased to be asked if he was a virgin). There was also *The Britannia* pub, where Sally, a member of the congregation, was the proprietor. It always reminded my father of drinking in Irish pubs in the 1930s. There was no bar for Sally to stand behind - patrons would sit in a semi-circle on red leather bench seats, and everyone would share in the conversation. I was convinced that our church hall would be an important part of our outreach, because of its situation - that made the work on its roof something of a priority, but how were we to raise the finance for it?

During my first Lent, which began two days after my Institution, we worked on the parable of the talents; I gave everyone in the congregation one pound, and told them to come back on Easter Day with more. I did not realise that the treasurer and wardens would count the resulting talents during the Easter Day sermon, and because of the proximity of the sacristy to the chancel, all I could hear was money being poured out on the desk as I preached on the gospel of the resurrection. I recall that we raised £700, which I announced at the end of the Mass. It was a terrific effort and we were all so enthusiastic - but later I had to point out that actually we had only raised half the amount required, and that there was no question of applying for a loan. When I had first met the Wardens, both Arthur Groves and Jack Evans said, 'Within reason you can do what you like but do not ever put us in a position where we have to borrow money.' 'Owe no man anything' was their motto and I honoured that. This left us in need of another income stream, if we were to reach out to the people.

In that first Lent I visited extensively, and came to know people in the pubs, clubs and shops, and in the hospital; as often as possible, I asked them how they would like to see the church become a more central part of the community. It was clear that for some time the clergy had been accepted as 'one of us' and the general pastoral care for everybody, especially in the hospital and the sick ministry and occasional offices, was greatly valued - but the option now emerged of creating a fellowship outside the worshipping community. It was being suggested that we should start a licensed club – the seventh such establishment in the proximity of the church. They also said they would like to help raise money with a weekly tote.

Early that summer we started the weekly tote; tickets were sold in pubs, clubs, and factories, businesses, and shops. Within a few weeks we were raising £200 a week, with a £100 pay-out - that was very good money in 1978. The tote was drawn after Sunday Evensong, in the rear room of the newly re-roofed hall. We had no licence, so we supplied beer and requested a donation, with a suggested guide price of 34p - the cost of a pint of Whitbread Tankard.

With at least £100 coming in each week, we were soon able to undertake other improvements in the hall. Availing ourselves of a Manpower Services Scheme for young people, we laid a new floor; Dave next door built a side extension to house the bar, and the rear room was panelled and began to look quite swish. Everything had to be done on the cheap. I rang the Magistrates' Clerk and explained that we had no money to employ a solicitor, so he invited me to go to the courts late one afternoon to fill in all the forms for the licence - which was granted quite swiftly. In addition, we were permitted to have twelve open events each year, which we could use for non-member nights or weddings.

We had so much fun in that club that I could write a short book about it. What excited me in particular was that we had many who were not members of the Church on our 'membership books', and on club nights (usually Fridays and Sundays) we had them mixing with our congregation and starting to ask questions. Occasionally some of them requested a hospital visit or came to Church, with some becoming committed members at our annual confirmation. At the Club and with the weekly tote, the comment most frequently heard was 'because we enjoy such things we expected the Church to be against us'. I was always careful to explain that the church was never actually against people, because God loves everybody. On the other hand, the Church can never condone irresponsible behaviour such as drunkenness and wild gambling. I asked them always to remember that joy and fellowship were two of the marks of the Christian community.

Thankfully, none of the pubs or the Labour Club saw us a rival, and many would have a drink with us and then go on to the Labour Club afterwards or vice versa. Christine and I went back twenty-eight years later for their St. Peter's night celebration, and I had to laugh when I saw two of my instructions in my bold handwriting still up in the bar!

We had some great social occasions in the parish: mention must be made of the 'Faggots and Peas' Suppers, the New Year's Eve Party with the Black Country Brass Band, and the St. Peter's Night party after the Mass. All these events attracted people who were not necessarily regular members of St. Peter's. The only drawback with the bar was if the rota broke down in some way. From time to time, at 6.30 on a Saturday night, the person responsible would ring in and say, 'Fr. Nick I'm very sorry I cannot work the bar tonight', and there was nothing for it but to turn out and do the duty.

I am grateful that cases of bad behaviour in the club were few. I remember one Saturday night pouring a full round of drinks for one wedding guest, and, as he took the tray away, he said that he would return to the bar to pay his debt. After he failed to come back, I told John Green, my fellow barman that night, that I would stop by and collect the money as I took a tray of drinks over to another table. John, with his usual smile and deep voice, said, 'I shouldn't, Father Nicholas, he looks as if he has had rather too much to drink.' I am afraid that when people take that kind of advantage of the church, it always makes me see red, so holding the tray, I went over and asked the guest to pay for his earlier drinks. He started to quibble, and then uttered some expletive, clenched his fist, and brought it up beneath the tray - all the drinks went flying over our new floor. Such occurrences were very rare.

There was little vandalism in the church and club, and only one case of thieving. This was largely because, in that community, the Church was something even petty criminals left alone because they knew that the Church cared for them. Furthermore, if anyone was found to have stolen from the Church, they would not be protected by others. Siphoning off fuel from Harry Hawkins yard or taking a tyre or two from it, was considered 'fair play' - but not taking from the Church.

Just after I returned from afternoon visiting late one November afternoon, a big department store in Wolverhampton rang me up and enquired whether I had lost any spirits from the club. They asked if I could go up and check, because the store detectives had stopped two of the lads on the Job Creation scheme on suspicion that they had stolen four big bottles of spirits. They swore they had not stolen them from the store, but confessed that they had taken them from our club. The employment scheme wanted to dismiss them, but I asked if they would reduce the penalty to a week with no wages, and then make them come to apologise to me. The last thing I wanted - given that finding jobs was so very hard - was for the Church to have ensured they did not find another job. We struck up a relationship with them, and, when they completed their time on the scheme, I regret we lost touch. With those on the employment scheme, and in so much of our ministry and life in the Church, we dare to hope that those we meet have been helped in some way by their time with us.

Unemployment became a very big issue, especially following the change of government in 1979, and many in the community and in the wider area were made redundant. John Marsh, one of my churchwardens - like so many of them there, one of the finest you could ever meet - was a foreman pipe fitter, and lost his job. I said to him that he would have to look elsewhere for employment, and if necessary move. He nearly blew a gasket, and said 'Nick if you want to be our priest never say that to anyone in Gornal.' His family had lived there for generations and the whole of his present family still lived in the neighbourhood; they would never move - and that was the same for everybody. They all cared for each other, and if their elderly were frail or sick, they would only allow them to go into the geriatric hospital (where I was the chaplain) at Burton Road as a last resort. Remembering that Burton Road had been the old workhouse many had promised their parents they would never put them in there.

Something similar happened with unemployment. It was regarded as 'in order' to accept money when they were on sick leave - which was known as being 'on the box' - but many of them said that, like their Dads, they would never 'take off the State'. I recall having heated arguments with several of them that it was their duty to 'sign on'. It still makes me very angry when many of those out of work or on any benefits are labelled by the popular press as 'scroungers' – in fact, there are still considerable numbers, like my parishioners, who refuse to take what they are entitled to. John the Warden found a job near Bristol - the firm's van would pick him up every day very early and he would be back for a late tea. I remember asking what he did in the back of the van on that long journey each day. 'It's a good time to pray, Nick.' If there was anything on at church in the evening, he would be there, finishing the evening with a few pints. Some twenty-three years later I was pleased to be able to offer him a last pint, shortly before he died, at Bishop's House, Blackburn, after my Installation and Enthronement.

I would put the growth in the congregation at that time down to three things. First, I had an excellent curate in Fr. Chris Marshall, who spoke with a broad Liverpudlian accent, was deeply prayerful, a brilliant preacher, and had a terrific sense of humour. He was totally loyal to me but would 'send me up', and he was wonderful with people. As the Church community, without being all self-conscious about it, we practised 'collaborative ministry', and just got on with it.

Secondly, we identified with the culture, and tried not to be six feet above it. Despite the poor state of the churchyard, what is called 'Churchyard Religion' was important to so many of the people. In my early days, I recall feeling slightly impatient when a sixty-year-old came up and apologised for not having tended the grave that week. Inside I felt, why does she not apologise for not coming to Mass. I came to appreciate that her 'sacred space', where she found a disclosure of God, was there with her husband whom she believed was 'at home with the Lord'. It is easy to dismiss this as primitive or 'folk religion', but it is the place from which some are starting - we realised that we would never bring them further on with the life of faith if we rubbished what was important to them at present. Of course, we didn't succeed with vast numbers, but they knew, not far away, was the God who cared about them, and His Church that would always welcome them.

The third aid to growth was through baptism. I talked through with the PCC the place of baptism, feeling strongly that if we could find a way that did not exclude anyone, but at the same time encouraged families to make an act of commitment to join the worshipping life of the Church, then we would be doing our best for those who came to baptism. This included pointing out that the promises made in baptism are the same as in confirmation; and that if parents were serious about the promises they made for their children they would think carefully about moving on to confirmation. We were fortunate in having a church community that was friendly to families, and we were prepared to give time to those preparing for the sacraments. Of course, not everyone responded; on one occasion I was reported to the bishop, and on another ended up in the daily West Midlands evening newspaper, *The Express and Star*, but the 'policy' was gentle and it worked, and new people came in this way.

Shortly after I went to Upper Gornal I attended the first Catholic Renewal in the Church of England Conference at what is now Loughborough University, which took place during Eastertide in 1978. Dr. Eric Kemp, Bishop of Chichester, was the mind behind the Conference, which was called because it was clear that the Catholic Movement in the Church of England needed re-galvanising. As always with Bishop Eric, this conference was carefully prepared; I was invited to meet him over dinner with others from five Midlands dioceses, to talk about where we hoped Catholic Renewal might take us, and what we should be giving our attention to at the Conference.

Although I was under the weather with 'flu, it was a good Conference, with over one thousand delegates, and very impressive major talks: Bishop Michael Marshall (Woolwich) on Creation, and Bishop Robert Terwilliger (Suffragan of Dallas) on Reconciliation. I always remember his saying that when he was a student, he went without lunch for a week to purchase Gustaf Aulen's *Christus Victor* and that since then, he had fed on it. The third major speaker – who followed a short address given to us by the then Archbishop of Canterbury, Dr. Donald Coggan - was Fr. Richard Holloway (then at Old St. Paul's Edinburgh) on Consecration. Not only was the theology utterly 'sound' but he presented it in a way that everyone could digest, and with such charisma - he was a star. Over the years, I devoured all his material, until he began to part company with the received tradition of the church. Subsequently, I purchased his autobiography,

Leaving Alexandria, A Memoir of Faith and Doubt (2012, Canongate Books Ltd), which helped me to understand why one with whom I closely identified for many years, took a radically different turning.

The worship at *Loughborough '78* was superb, with good sermons, and excellent input on the 'Social Gospel', mainly through the Jubilee Group, and notably through Fr. Ken Leech - then Rector of St. Matthew's Bethnal Green, who, in his retirement, made helpful visits to us in Blackburn Diocese. I was also pleased to meet, at a regional group meeting, Bishop Mark Green, Bishop of Aston in the Diocese of Birmingham, who, many years later, was to become a colleague and good friend.

There were others there, like Mark, who were not the 'usual Anglo-Catholic suspects', including: Bishop Robert Runcie (soon to be Archbishop of Canterbury), Bishop Colin James (Wakefield), and Fr. Richard Harries (then Vicar of All Saints' Fulham and later Bishop of Oxford). Certainly, the subject of the Ordination of Women received an airing, with the case against clearly and carefully argued in a fine paper from the ecumenist Canon Roger Greenacre, who had recently been appointed a Residentiary Canon of Chichester Cathedral. The strongest speech in favour, I seem to recall, was Sister Carol from the Malvern sisters. However, the subject did not dominate the Conference, and Catholics were on both sides of the argument. While we realised that there might well be difficult times ahead on this issue, the Oxford

Movement today was adapting to the post-conciliar Church, and keen to take forward, into the last quarter of the twentieth century, what the Fathers of the Oxford Movement had bequeathed.

There was good follow-up to the Conference. In Lichfield Diocese we joined with Birmingham and Worcester dioceses; Fr. Bryan Parry, Vicar of St. Gregory's, Small Heath, was the Chair of the Regional Committee, and I became its Secretary. We organised a day conference in the Autumn of 1979, taking over Birmingham Town Hall; Fr. Richard Holloway came down on the night sleeper from Edinburgh to address us, and Bishop Hugh Montefiore, Bishop of Birmingham, was the chief celebrant at the Mass.

We began to see a few cracks beginning to appear as to what qualified one to be a Catholic Anglican. Bishop Montefiore was certainly a liberal Catholic and liked to 'fly a few kites' - and he frequently found himself attracting headlines. Consequently some representatives asked for Bishop Mark Green, the Suffragan in the Diocese, to be the principal celebrant. Fortunately, this was not allowed to gather a head of steam - after all, at a Catholic celebration one can hardly lock the diocesan bishop out of Mass in his own diocese when we are all in full communion with him. As always, Hugh celebrated the Mass with great dignity and was most gracious about the event.

In Wolverhampton we had our own, more local celebration at St. Martin's Church, with the diocesan,

Bishop Kenneth Skelton, as the principal celebrant and Fr. Kenneth Leech as the main speaker. So, around 1980, it seemed that Catholic Renewal had certainly taken root in the Catholic Wing - with Jubilee Groups focussing on social issues, groups for prayer and study, and even renewed missions, all springing up. In 1979 the retired Archbishop of Canterbury, Dr. Ramsey, went to Walsingham for the National Pilgrimage, as did the new Archbishop of Canterbury, Dr Runcie, in 1981 - and with the Anglican-Roman Catholic International Commission making progress, I wondered if Catholics in the Church of England might not again be in the ascendant.

Life was extremely busy in the parish, not least with the additional hospital chaplaincy work. Although we always took our holidays as a family, I was not good about taking a full day off each week. Years later, when I was making a first visit to all the deaneries in Blackburn Diocese, a priest asked me at an open session, 'Will you model good working practice and take your day off and adequate rest periods?' I could not give a very satisfactory answer - and I do thank Christine and Claire for putting up with my being out so much. Christine was very good about it, not least because it was much the same for many other clergy at that time. I would certainly advise clergy now to guard their family time, but without surrendering to the creeping 'hours of work' mentality which some clergy are adopting in the light of Clergy Terms of Service legislation.

Burton Road Hospital, on the edge of the parish, had a modern Intensive Care Unit (ITU), a Maternity Unit, a Geriatric Unit, and a Psychiatric Unit. I shared the chaplaincy with the Vicar of St. James's, Eve Hill - he had responsibility for the ITU and the Maternity Unit, and I had the rest. The hospital threatened to take pastoral oversight of the Psychiatric Unit away from me, because I did some occupational therapy with the patients, and managed to put most things together the wrong way - so I was asked to limit my involvement to visiting.

In my first month we started a Friday Mass each week for the whole hospital - some three patients came and one of the Ward Sisters, who was a member of St. Peter's; I also used to bring Lottie from one of the estates, a very faithful blind person who came to the daily Mass at the church - and that was the congregation. One Friday morning, on our way to the hospital, Lottie broke the news to me that Pope John Paul I had died after reigning only 38 days - and so began the Year of the Three Popes.

We started taking regular communion to the wards, but there was no tabernacle in the Chapel. I went to see the Hospital Administrator and asked if the carpenter could make me a tabernacle; we would also need a Sanctuary lamp and the Altar pulled out from the wall. The Administrator, as always, was most helpful. I trained up three parishioners to be chaplain's assistants, so we could cover more of the patients. I was always given a session with new nursing staff and regularly lunched in the hospital canteen, not just to get a cheap meal, but to sit and get to know staff and their needs. This was the time when the hospital was building up its occupational therapy work, and I recall one Friday when I could not be at the Chapel Mass, that I enquired of the curate how many people were there that morning - and he smiled and said they couldn't get them all in. I laughed and he said that I would see for myself the following Friday.

When I was in the hospital, early the following week, I went into one of the geriatric wards and the patients, who were usually sitting in their chairs in serried ranks, this time were all in a circle and engaged in some activity. I met Marion the new Head Occupational Therapist, and she explained how things would be done in future, and she added that the chaplaincy had a part to play. She wanted to see more of us on the wards, more services, and helpers to wheel people to the small chapel. In addition to the Friday Mass, which was now full every week, we started a Monday Mass on one of the wards. We certainly found the work increasing, which was a bit of a problem for the new curate, who could not stand the sight of blood. June Williams, and the other lay assistants, were lovely with the patients - and if they had not joined the team, we could not have taken advantage of the new opportunities that presented themselves to us.

The hospital closed some five years after I left. I was asked by the Administrator shortly before my departure to look at the plans for the new Russells

Hall Hospital, which was to be thoroughly 'state-of-the-art'. I tried to look intelligent as I scanned them, but after about five minutes I could not see the chapel and enquired where it was. The omission was corrected. I have always enjoyed hospital work, and very seriously considered becoming a full-time hospital chaplain at one stage. I was pleased, when I became an archdeacon, that the bishop made me Bishop's Adviser for Hospital Chaplaincy in the whole of the Diocese of Chichester. Indeed, my very last function, just before I was consecrated Bishop, was to return from Blackburn to The Conquest Hospital in Hastings for the chaplains' annual meeting, always an enjoyable occasion. A decade later, when I would next walk through the doors of that hospital, was not such a happy occasion.

Some have asked how I became a diocesan bishop, when I only ever worked in parishes before becoming an archdeacon. It is true that of the diocesan bishops in my time I had been in a parish longer than anyone else. Although always based in a parish, I was fortunate to experience other sector ministries and spheres of work - nevertheless, I ask what better experience and preparation is there for the chief pastor in a diocese than being a parish priest? My colleagues had held various other posts, including diocesan missioners, university lecturers, chaplains to universities or to schools, chaplains to bishops, worked overseas, run missionary societies, principals of theological colleges or on the staff of theological colleges, and cathedral canons and the occasional dean of a cathedral. A very few, like me, had been archdeacons, and many had been suffragan bishops. The House of Bishops is supposed to be very broadly based, which is right. I suspect we might find that this will become less the case with recent changes to the appointments system.

Apart from teaching in a parish or clergy context, the only formal teaching post I had was in 1980 as a tutor in liturgy on the Gilmore Course for deaconesses at Queen's College Birmingham - and I only had one student, Hazel. Although it meant reading quite extensively, and not just mugging up a few notes from university and Mirfield days, I enjoyed the work, and the sessions with Hazel. I am not an academic liturgist, but I have always kept abreast of liturgical thinking, and was honoured to serve as Chairman of the Diocesan Liturgical Committee some years later, in Chichester. When I was elected to the General Synod in 1995 I was asked to join the Liturgical Commission, and perhaps unwisely declined the invitation as, at that time, I could not afford the time to become too heavily involved in the life of the Synod.

To my surprise, I was told that I was once considered for a post as a pastoral tutor at a theological college but it was thought wrong to invite me to apply, as I had only recently moved to a new parish. I am sure it was right to leave me in parishes, and perhaps I was able to make my contribution to the training of clergy through having ordination candidates on placement every year for some nine years. I was also given deacons and newly-ordained priests to train over many years.

The last major part of our five-year plan at St. Peter's
was to have a School of Prayer, which Fr. Simon
Holden (1930-2019), a monk from the Community of
the Resurrection, ran for us. As always, with anything
Mirfield does, it was carefully prepared and there was
much prayerful support. Simon made a preliminary
visit some nine months in advance, and then preached
Holy Week for us – so, by the time the School started,
he was well known.

Before joining the Community of the Resurrection,
Simon was a curate in Middlesbrough, and knew
what parishes like St. Peter's were about; he was at
home in the Labour Club and our Social Club, and
people would open up to him. His preaching and
talks were very accessible. There were major 'teach-
ins' every day, and, in addition to the daily services,
there was an introduction to various forms of prayer, a
vigil, and opportunities for confession and absolution.
Additionally, there was a half day with the deanery
clergy, and, on the final Saturday, the usual St. Peter's
Supper. What brought joy to my heart was that in
so many ways it was all rather like the old-fashioned
mission, with people who were not regulars coming
along each evening.

I organised a similar School in Mayfield, my next parish,
with Fr. Andrew Norton, CR, who had been a parish
priest for many years before joining the Community;
and another in Eastbourne, with Bishop Colin Docker,
the recently-retired Bishop of Horsham, who had been
one of my predecessors in the parish. In those two

parishes, I was privileged to stay long enough after the Schools of Prayer to see the difference they made to the 'spiritual temperature' of the parish and the signs that lives had really been changed.

Unfortunately, I was not at St. Peter's long enough after the School to gauge any change – because, on the Sunday following Fr. Simon's departure, I had to announce that I was leaving to become Vicar of Mayfield, in my home county of East Sussex. The story of how I ended up going there after four-and-a-quarter years in Gornal is a long one. By that time I had spent just under nine years in and around the Black Country of the West Midlands, where I had been so happy ministering and where we had been happy living among such wonderful people.

I was sorry, also, to say farewell to Bishop Kenneth Skelton, the Diocesan Bishop. I admired him in many ways; he took time to get to know his clergy and was generous with the time and encouragement he gave to me as a young incumbent. Although he came across as shy initially, I found him very easy - and it helped that he could always see the humour in situations. He had the gift of drawing out the best in people. He was a truly pastoral bishop, who worked collaboratively and strategically. This remarkably gifted man, whose leadership was prophetic, appears to have been forgotten about in the Church of England - possibly because he was a very humble person.

Kenneth had served as Bishop of Matabeleland from

1962 to 1970 in western Rhodesia, where he was deeply respected as a pastor and theologian, and where he championed the cause of the black majority, inevitably clashing with many politicians. He wrote a gripping account of his ministry in Matabeleland, *Bishop in Smith's Rhodesia* (Mambo Press, 1985). The Law and Order Minister called him 'The Devil's Advocate', and stated that the government was watching him. He was also dubbed 'Red Skelton,' after the American comedian. Some commented that Kenneth could best be compared in the Church of England with Bishop George Bell, for both worked tirelessly for social justice and were fearless in speaking out.

Although Bishop Kenneth was much too wise to talk openly about my medium- and longer-term future, or to dangle possible posts in front of me, he was keen that I should broaden the scope of my ministry. The nearest I came to a 'falling out' with him was when I accepted my new post in Chichester Diocese. However, just before I left, I wrote and asked him for permission to invite our old friend Bishop John Daly, former Bishop of Korea, to confirm. His reply was, 'No, I will come myself'. Consequently, a week before we left, we had an enjoyable supper in the vicarage followed by a wonderful Confirmation Eucharist, and a party afterwards in the Club. It was with real sadness that I said 'good-bye' to him; he was a remarkable bishop in so many ways, he seemed to understand what I was doing in the parish, and he knew me at a deep level. In different circumstances, he would have made an excellent spiritual director for me.

6   THE CALL TO THE SOUTH, MAYFIELD

We moved into Mayfield Vicarage in the second week of February in 1982. As we thought about the move, we realised this was going to mean significant changes for all of us - not least for Claire, now aged four, as there was no local authority nursery education available, and she had to go back to play school until September when she started school.

While Sussex was home to me, Christine and I seriously wondered if the Bishop of Lichfield might have been right, and I should have continued in the West Midlands. My first three churches had been in economically-deprived areas; Mayfield and Five Ashes presented something of a contrast. The previous churchwarden at Mayfield had been Glubb Pasha (Lt. Gen. Sir John Glubb) and the congregation included many very distinguished retired people, some whom continued to occupy prominent positions. My first 'run-in' was with someone who had previously been married to a cabinet minister in Harold Macmillan's government. I recall talking to two guests at a dinner party, both of whom were recalling their Cambridge days, and they asked me if I was keeping quiet because 'I had been to the other place.' They were somewhat disconcerted when I said 'another place, and it was red brick - one of the first red brick universities'.

It was clear immediately that, as with the Black Country of the West Midlands, no one minded who you were, so long as you were genuine. I had actually been to two prep schools and a kindergarten in Sussex, and one of the PCC members had served with a cousin of mine in the Gurkhas. Because I spoke clearly in church without a regional accent, the very few who were concerned about social standing had few concerns about the new Vicar. They were pleased to have a young Vicar (35) with a warm and friendly wife, whose father was Dean of York, and a happy and publicly well-behaved daughter who would go to the local school.

The institution took place during a Eucharist and was presided over by the Area Bishop of Lewes. Keble College, Oxford held the patronage of the living, so I was therefore presented to the bishop by the college chaplain, the Revd. Dr. Geoffrey Rowell (1943-2017), later Bishop of Gibraltar in Europe. After I was consecrated, we became good friends - I learnt much from him and have consulted him on many occasions. We made common cause on a number of wider church issues. Sadly, he died early in retirement and his wisdom, kindness and friendship are greatly missed.

The Archdeacon of Lewes and Hastings, the Ven. Max Godden, inducted me. He was very 'old school', but with a keen sense of humour and, although trained at an Anglo-Catholic theological college, made it clear that he would rather Mayfield was a little 'lower down the candle'. Before the service, looking towards the altar outside the sacristy door, with its tabernacle, traditional six candle sticks, and other outward trappings, he said to me 'I gather this place is rather different from where you've come from', expecting me to say something about the demography of Upper Gornal. I responded, 'Oh yes, archdeacon, this is rather more low church.' He really liked that, and had a good laugh. He became a great source of encouragement to me and a wise counsellor.

The reception after the institution was held in the cloister of the Roman Catholic convent school, which was next door to the churchyard. St. Dunstan's worked closely with the convent and the school, and this generous invitation was indeed a sign of the beginning of a special relationship for us personally with the Society of the Holy Child, Jesus and with the convent school which, in a small but rich way, still continues today.

I had always tried to live out the traditional priestly day: prayer, Divine Office, Mass, and office work in the morning; visiting in the afternoon; then the evening meal, following Evensong; and after that, parish activities or more visiting or desk work, and possibly time for relaxation. Accordingly, on my first afternoon, I started off down West Street at two o'clock to visit Sir John and Lady Glubb; there was no answer. I went to a couple of other houses in that area of the parish, and again, no answer. I came across a Roman Catholic I had met the previous evening and told her that I could not gain access to several houses. She kindly pointed out that people would have been enjoying an afternoon rest, but suggested that I went up to the Memorial Hall where the afternoon Women's Institute was meeting. I pushed the door open. Everyone stopped talking and looked at me, amazed that the new vicar, on his first afternoon, had come to see them. I 'worked the room', made sure I spoke to everybody, and stayed for tea and a piece of cake. When someone told me the name of their dog, and I met her dog walking the very next day and also greeted the dog by name, I was off to a very fine beginning in the parish.

I visited as much as I could in the first weeks, despite the afternoon closed doors. After my first Sunday, when a couple of church members, who had been at the Institution, had not attended, I decided to visit them late on Monday morning, and enquired as tactfully as possible, if all was well. The parishioner received me most courteously, but explained they could not come every Sunday, particularly if they were entertaining at lunch time - I was not to use up my precious time visiting them, and we would be invited round to dinner. I soon learnt that 'the ever-open door' approach of St. Peter's Upper Gornal and my other parishes, was not the way of Mayfield and Five Ashes. I also learnt whom it was safe to visit in a casual way - as for the others, I would ring them up to enquire when I could come. I gave the highest priority to going to see parishioners in hospitals.

One of the issues facing me as parish priest was liturgical. *The Alternative Service Book (1980)* (ASB) had not been implemented, and a form of *Alternative Services*, series 3 was still in use. Any attempt to raise this matter would have been construed as an open invitation to discuss either the absence of the 1662 Book of Common Prayer (BCP) in Sunday services, or making the churchmanship of St. Dunstan's more obviously 'middle of the road'. I therefore tried a more oblique approach. For my first Lent I decided to give a series of talks on a Wednesday evening on the development of the liturgy including an introduction to the *Alternative Service Book*.

In the Summer we produced a simple Mass book which was basically ASB with no frills, although we put in the usual additions you would expect in a Catholic parish. We agreed that once a month the 12.15 Eucharist would be BCP, and Sung Evensong would also be 1662. At the next Annual Parochial Church Meeting I emphasised that we had now made a decision, and that the worship debate was therefore over until such time as the ASB was revised - which thankfully was not until the year 2000.

Most of the congregation said they were heartily glad that I had taken a very clear and firm line – even if it meant a tiny handful went to a neighbouring parish for Sunday morning 1662. Eventually the 12.15 BCP congregation dwindled to one person, a retired Rear Admiral. With characteristic generosity he rang me up and said, 'Padre you've better things to be doing on a Sunday after three services - I'll start coming to the 10.45'. As we were blessed with the finest of choirs, under the direction of Kenneth Pont, the Gloria, the Sanctus and Benedictus and Agnus Dei were sung to a variety of settings often in Latin, most Sundays. The hymns and the Lord's Prayer were always in the traditional versions – so, for the most part, the '1662 brigade' were content with that.

Another issue was the poor level of financial giving. My previous parish was part of an Urban Priority Area, where Margaret Thatcher's economic policy was beginning to hit hard and unemployment was rising at an alarming rate, but the church always paid its Parish Share (the Common Fund to pay the stipends of the clergy, to house them, and to meet the cost of all the other services that are provided centrally) to the Diocese. It therefore seemed absurd that I had arrived in what was one of the wealthiest areas in the country and that there was a £8,500 deficit on the Quota (Share).

I immediately set about running a home-spun Stewardship Campaign, and was delighted to tell the parishioners, most of whom were endowed with a generous proportion of this world's goods, how their giving was poorer than in my previous parish, between Dudley and Wolverhampton. I attempted to help them to see that 'giving in grace' is part of our worship. The archdeacon gave us two years to clear the deficit, but – amazingly - it was achieved in six months. Some three years later we had a traditional Stewardship Campaign with the Diocesan Stewardship Officer, and we treated it as a Mission; amongst other benefits, this ensured greater future financial security for the day-to-day running of the parish.

In my second week, I took the Sister Superior of the convent out for a pub lunch. The Religious Order was progressive, founded by Cornelia Connelly, an ex-Anglican, and their way of life was basically Jesuit. The Superior herself was somewhat radical. I enquired whether Christine (who had been Head of Religious Education in an Independent School, a Grammar School and a Comprehensive School) might ever have the opportunity to apply for a post at their school. Gently and firmly the answer was No. Indeed, this excellent school did not even offer 'A' level Religious Studies. We never thought any more about it.

Eighteen months after that conversation, I was talking to one of the sisters about an Anglican girl at the school whom I was preparing for confirmation. I happened to drop into the conversation that Christine had taught 'A' level Religious Studies. The next day she enquired whether Christine would tutor this girl for her 'A' level Religious Studies course. There was just one condition - that she be taught at the Vicarage. Christine readily agreed, and was looking forward to teaching again, even if it was just one student; we thought the remuneration would be something like a box of chocolates at the end of the course. The following day the same nun came down to say, 'You know, this will be fully salaried.' The next year Christine had several girls to teach, and, a couple of years after that, she moved into a school class room - and continued to teach there until we left for Blackburn. When she was eleven, in our second year in Eastbourne, Claire went to the school as a weekly boarder and was very happy there.

Each year I used to prepare groups of Anglican girls for confirmation. A number of the girls sang in the church choir, and the convent school choirs took part in our concerts several times a year. My predecessor, Canon Donald Carter, with the local Roman Catholic priest, had inaugurated a shared Roman Catholic-Anglican Easter Vigil in the convent chapel, celebrating everything together except for the eucharistic liturgy. For this part of the service we Anglicans would move to the altar in the Ante Chapel, usually managing to reach the Lord's words of institution simultaneously. Afterwards the convent would provide its most generous hospitality.

In my second year I arranged an evening in the convent for Anglicans and Roman Catholics in Sussex to come together for a progress report from the Anglican-Roman Catholic International Commission. (ARCIC) which had been established by Pope Paul VI and Archbishop Michael Ramsey. An Anglican bishop on the commission and the Roman Catholic joint-secretary introduced a fascinating evening. With such encouraging ecumenical work going on locally, Mayfield was the right place to hold this event.

We were fortunate that the Roman Catholic co-chair of ARCIC was the local Roman Catholic bishop, subsequently Cardinal, Cormac Murphy O'Connor. He and the Anglican Bishop of Chichester, Dr. Eric Kemp, then Chairman of the Faith and Order Advisory Group, had worked together on ARCIC material. They produced joint study materials for both the Anglican and Roman Catholic Dioceses, so that we could work through the documents together. I was invited by Bishop Eric to lead the initiative in East Sussex; this included a one-day conference in Eastbourne chaired by Bishop Cormac, with whom I had spent a little time in 1974, when I visited the English College in Rome when he was its Rector. These were exciting times ecumenically, especially in relations with the Roman Catholic Church. They were heady ecumenical days in Mayfield, with so many activities engaged in jointly - and I have maintained the friendships that were forged at that time. Sadly we appear to have stumbled back into an ecumenical winter, but I remain confident that God will, in His time, bring something more from the great gains that were made in those earlier days.

In 1983, the 150th anniversary of the Oxford Movement was celebrated, and Mayfield - as a Keble College, Oxford living - was invited to participate in the procession at the Thanksgiving Eucharist in Oxford at which the Archbishop of Canterbury, Dr. Runcie, was the principal celebrant. In that year, also, the second Catholic Renewal Conference took place. Some good preparatory reading material was sent to all participants, including *Hearts not Garments* by Michael Hollings (a Roman Catholic parish priest) and *Signs of Glory* by Richard Holloway (then serving at The Advent Church in Boston). I remember Loughborough 1983 less well than the 1978 Conference. Fr. Michael Hollings spoke passionately about ministry in the inner city, and the Abbot of Nashdom, Dom Wilfred Weston, called for a renewed vision for Catholicism in the Church of England. Bishop Eric Kemp spoke memorably and with unwonted passion in launching the Church Union Anniversary Appeal.

The debate about the future possible ordination of women to the priesthood had moved up a gear. All in all, I did not come away with the same degree of enthusiasm as after 1978. Some years later, I enquired of a priest what he felt came out of the 1983 conference, and his reply was 'Loughborough '83 was sunk without trace in a tide of gin and tonic'. I believe that was an unfair assessment. The Anniversary Appeal enabled grants for promising projects to be made to Catholic parishes for many years. I am also confident that without those two Renewal Conferences - and the spin-offs from them - Catholics in the Church of England would have been in a much weaker position at the end of the 1980s and early 1990s. Indeed, we may well have found ourselves in a worse position in the drawing up of the legislation to permit women to be ordained to the priesthood, resulting in a more unsatisfactory settlement for traditionalists afterwards.

David Besant was churchwarden throughout the whole of my time in Mayfield, and I met him regularly. He was a London solicitor, then working in Tunbridge Wells, and we would generally meet in a country pub outside the town for lunch. He had served on the General Synod, was very wise, probably a bit over cautious, but with a good handle on what was happening, and still very friendly with Donald Carter, a previous vicar, then at Christ Church, Leonards-on-Sea as Rector. I admired what Donald had done both in Mayfield and at Christ Church, St. Leonards, and, without ever interfering, he was most helpful to me - particularly when he encouraged me to stay on in Mayfield when, three years after I arrived, the bishop offered me a positively 'mouth-watering' post.

David was also very generous, taking me with him on the diocesan pilgrimage to Chartres. The other churchwarden, George Welbourne, had been a director of education in London, and, like David, was most generous and supportive. He and I drew up plans for a major reordering of the churchyard. Once again, I made contact with the Manpower Services Commission, and they were prepared to make this a twelve-month unemployment scheme. Unfortunately, in undertaking the works, George and I had misread the section concerning kerbstones in the Chancellor of the Diocese's Churchyard Regulations, and the local amenities society had noticed the infringement, and consulted a local barrister, also a Q.C.

One of the shopkeepers in the village, with whom we were on very good terms, came over to the vicarage one afternoon in tears and hugged Christine and said, 'You know the vicar may go to prison for this oversight.' The Chancellor of the Diocese (the chief legal officer) did come down to visit the churchyard, but in the end chose not to hear the case in a Consistory Court; he met the objectors - who started raising their voices at one stage (very out of character for Mayfield) - and finally granted a confirmatory faculty. Had we not managed to have the Manpower Scheme I have no idea how we could ever have afforded and undertaken this huge project.

Launching the Tower and Bells Appeal, in Mayfield with the actress Jenny Seagrove (1986).

When talking with the churchwardens in my early days, we spoke about what we ought to tackle during my years in Mayfield. Jokingly, George said, 'Well the bells have not been rung for thirteen years and the spire needs re-shingling, the tower re-pointing and other works in that area, all of which would cost around £150,000'. We set to, and the whole community responded generously, and raised the money quite swiftly. Although many residents of Mayfield and Five Ashes had considerable resources, and we did receive some quite large sums, I never recall any donation over four figures. (The dedication of the work by the Bishop of Lewes took place on Sat 8 December 1987, and the next day I had to announce that the Bishop had appointed me Vicar and Rural Dean of Eastbourne.)

As at St. Peter's Upper Gornal, each summer I continued to receive two ordinands on placement for two weeks from the College of the Resurrection, Mirfield; they lived with us in the vicarage, shadowed me, and were assigned certain duties. I enjoyed these weeks, which provided an opportunity for me to get to know how training for the priesthood was developing, and what I should be reading. Mirfield usually sent me students who had to readjust to life in Mayfield; during a hot summer I had to suggest to one student that he might be better received if he did not walk around in a vest when he was not wearing his cassock. Having told another about an invitation to dinner at which the other guests were Oxbridge graduates, he was concerned, as he had only been to the North Staffordshire Polytechnic. I told him that his host had been at Brasenose College, Oxford - often known as BNC - and that, if asked where he studied, he should simply reply 'at NSP'; I told him they would smile politely at this - and they did.

All the students who visited the parish, from whatever background, were received very warmly, and found most of the people they visited forward-looking: they acknowledged that the world was changing, and many demonstrated rare insight. Equally, the ministry of the ordinands was much appreciated by the parish.

I enjoyed the voluntary support of two 'part-time' retired curates during my incumbency; I also had an ordinand from Westcott House for a year, before he was ordained, and one from the Aston Training Scheme for six months, before he went to Mirfield. The Bishop of Lewes sent me young men who were members of his scheme for young people, a couple of whom went on to be ordained, and one who later came to me as a curate in Eastbourne, in 1988.

Having ordinands around enlivened the parish - they encouraged the engagement of young people, aged seventeen and eighteen and even a few older ones, all eager to grow in faith - and always full of fun. They gave me a great fortieth birthday party, and wrote a song for me. We sometimes went to the Middle House hotel opposite the church for a drink after Sunday Evensong, and, one snowy night, knowing I did not like walking on the snow and ice, they took me, clad in my cassock, back to the vicarage on a sledge – which unfortunately tipped over.

The members of the young people's group knew that they lived in a privileged area - they often enquired about the West Midlands and my first three parishes. We decided to go for a weekend to the great Anglo-Catholic parish I had known for many years, St. James', Wednesbury, where there was a very active parish priest, with considerable organisational skills. I told him I wanted him to arrange a weekend for ten young people, centred around the church's worship, that would give them a good introduction to the life and mission of the church in an area of high unemployment, where the local industries were closing.

It was a real education for them, and they engaged keenly in every activity - and with the people. They each stayed in a different house in the parish and enjoyed most generous hospitality. For me, it was one of the most enriching weekends of my whole ministry. Thirty-five years on, that great flagship church of Black Country Anglo-Catholicism, has been closed, to the sorrow of very many people - although doubtless there were practical reasons for it. In arriving at a decision to close such a church we surely need to look beyond John Betjeman's 'waking days when faith was taught and fanned to a golden blaze'. In that and countless other communities, God, through His Church, stood with the people in their hardship; and many heard His promise that perseverance through difficult times would win an eternal reward. Perhaps the Church needs to search for a possible reason to retain some of its great centres of worship as living signs of what the parish ministry has accomplished in the past.

While in Mayfield, I began to paint on a wider canvas. I did not spend much time at Diocesan Church House as I was only on the Diocesan Stewardship committee and the Diocesan Pastoral committee, but to my great surprise, after less than nine months in the parish, I was also appointed Rural Dean of Dallington. The clergy were informed that the ballot papers were for consultation purposes, but the bishop assured me that I was, in fact, elected by the deanery clergy. I expect it was because I was the youngest. This meant I now had to divide my time between working in the deanery and in the parish.

I enjoyed going around the parishes, in what was probably the most rural deanery in the whole of East Sussex. I helped them in whatever way they required, and presided over the Deanery Synod and the Clergy Chapter. I also represented them at meetings with the bishop and archdeacon and the Pastoral Committee.

I remember arriving for my first archdeaconry rural deans' meeting, which took place at the area bishop's house. The next youngest rural dean was twenty years older than me, and the others were in their sixties. I walked in, not knowing most of them, as I was still new to the diocese and a bit hesitant; then Bill Peters, Rural Dean of Uckfield, a great cricketer, and former Chaplain of Brighton College, came across and nearly shook my hand off, as he said, 'Welcome brother to the best club in East Sussex.' From then on, I felt at home with them all, and usually looked forward to the bi-monthly meetings. Once a year, all the rural deans from the whole diocese met with the diocesan bishop at the Bishop's Palace, which was a more formal occasion.

Towards the end of our time in Mayfield, Christine was appointed secretary to the Diocesan Clergy Wives, and enjoyed enormously working with Pat Kemp, the Bishop's wife, striking up a warm friendship with her.

When I was moving to Mayfield, I was concerned about my limited knowledge of music, because at the time the parish was a centre of musical excellence - and has continued to be so. I told the Director of Music that I wanted music to support the liturgy, and was keen for music to serve the mission of outreach. I need not have worried – and I went on to enjoy a very positive working and personal relationship with Kenneth Pont, the Director of Music (who also became Head of Music at the convent school).

The church, the school, the Friends of Music in Mayfield, and the local community, worked very closely together to present the Mayfield Festival of Music and the Arts, which lasted a fortnight in alternate years. Many distinguished artists were invited to take part in the Festival. The first person to sign our new visitors book was Gustav Leonhardt, the Dutch harpsichordist and conductor, who stayed with us after his recital. The final choral concert was always conducted by Sir David Wilcocks; afterwards he would have a bath in the vicarage, followed, usually, by a reception in our garden.

One year, John Tinsley, our old Professor from the Department of Theology at Leeds University - subsequently Bishop of Bristol - presided and preached at the Festival Mass and gave an illustrated lecture on the iconography of the atonement. The other delightful house guest that weekend was Mary Wilson, wife of the former Prime Minister. Her poetry had been set to music by Malcolm Williamson, the Master of the Queen's Music, who was present at the performance. During those years, I came to appreciate music, and greatly regretted that I had not taken earlier opportunities to enjoy it, to learn to play a musical instrument – and to sing better.

I did enjoy being a country parish priest and rural dean, and felt just as comfortable working in a parish like Mayfield as in Wolverhampton and Dudley. We liked the people (as was the case in all our parishes), and several of them from Mayfield have remained in touch and become good friends. My two successors have kindly invited me to return from time to time. Fr. Nigel Prior graciously permitted Claire to be married by me in the church (spectacularly decorated by two friends, Sheila Humphrey and Alison Brilliant) shortly after I became Bishop of Blackburn, with Bishop Mark Green (former Bishop of Aston) preaching - a great family friend, to whom I owe so much.

After six years in Mayfield we moved fifteen miles, even further south, to Eastbourne, where I had been appointed Vicar of the Parish Church and Rural Dean. At forty-one years of age, I became the youngest Vicar of Eastbourne for a hundred and fifty years. For over seventy-five years every other Vicar of Eastbourne had gone on to be a Suffragan Bishop, and my immediate predecessor had gone into retirement - so rather too many said that they knew what my next post would be. When I responded that I had the stamp of parish priest right through me - like Blackpool rock - I really believed it. Certainly, I looked forward to a long stint in my fifth parish.

7   DOWN TO THE COAST. THE EASTBOURNE YEARS

Upon arrival in Eastbourne, our first task was to co-operate in the building of a new home in the grounds of the original Eastbourne Vicarage in Glebe Close. Among the former Vicars of Eastbourne was Canon William Streatfeild - later Bishop of Lewes, and father to the children's author Noel Streatfeild, who died only a year before we arrived. In the grounds of the new vicarage was the gravestone of her dog, Spot. Three of Noel's books had become films, including *Ballet Shoes*. She also wrote three semi-autobiographical novels: *A Vicarage Family, Away from the Vicarage* and *Beyond the Vicarage*. At the age of fourteen, Claire, having endured yet another Sunday lunch with at least one clerical guest, announced she would one day 'tell all' and write the fourth novel about Eastbourne Vicarage.

Eastbourne Parish Church (St. Mary's, Old Town) - even though it was a little outside the new Town Centre - was a very active church, with all the usual parish activities and, as the Civic Church, was very involved in the life of the community and town. The church had an extensive electoral roll and an excellent congregation for the Sunday Parish Eucharist. It was not 'smells and bells', rather what used to be known as 'Prayer Book Catholic', and the wardens said the mind of the congregation was that there should be no major change in that tradition. There had been a daily morning Eucharist at eight o'clock since the beginning of the twentieth century, and the Blessed Sacrament had been perpetually reserved since then; the daily Offices were said publicly, and a few parishioners availed themselves of the Sacrament of Reconciliation (Confession).

Each Sunday there were always three Eucharists, with an additional monthly Family Service, and full Choral Evensong with sermon at 6.30. There were plenty of requests for baptism, and holy matrimony - sometimes three on a Saturday. There were many sick communicants, and Eucharists were also celebrated in nursing homes.

Initially, I enjoyed generous clerical support in the parish: I had a deputy vicar - Fr. Don Cluer, who had a few years to serve before retirement - and a curate, straight from college. We had a number of retired priests, who would willingly assist; and Fr. Tony Windross, a self-supporting priest in secular employment, who had been trained in the parish. He was on the liberal wing of the church theologically - unusually among our curates - and went on to become a parish priest successively in East Grinstead, in Sheringham and in Hythe. His last full-time appointment was near Bude, where he was also Area Dean - he is currently priest-in-charge of Pevensey and Pevensey Bay. He and his wife Pat have been good friends, and it has been an encouragement to see his ministry blossom over the years. We also had the services of a Reader (Alf Davy, a former Church Army officer), a full-time verger (who lived in the flat in the Old Parsonage), and a paid secretary. We were blessed with many able and keen volunteers, who took lay ministry seriously. In so many respects it was an ideal parish.

For many years, the Vicar of Eastbourne was also Rural Dean of Eastbourne. The archdeacon told me that he and the bishop would divide the functions specific to their offices in the deanery, but he added 'in effect, Nicholas, you are Bishop, Archdeacon and Rural Dean of Eastbourne rolled into one'. The news was rather daunting for a young man coming in from the country, and to begin with I was the youngest incumbent, once again - and there were some very strong-minded clergy in the deanery. Over half of them were confirmed Anglo-Catholics, and a third committed Evangelicals, and only a couple were what might be called 'middle of the road.' Needless to say, the Clergy Chapter was often very lively.

I was instituted by the area bishop, and, as we processed out, the archdeacon said, in a quiet voice, 'you can still go back to Mayfield, it's not too late to change your mind'. If it was a joke, it provoked only a hollow laugh. We really had enjoyed Mayfield, and here was I taking on a big job, which in all honesty was rather too early for me, even though I was flattered that the bishop and his staff believed I was up to it. The reception was held on two floors of the Towner Art Gallery, because the parish meeting room in the Old Parsonage was not large enough. I was pleased about that, because it was a sign that my ministry was to be wider than just to the parish, encompassing not only other churches in the deanery but the wider life of this ever-developing seaside town.

As with the four other parishes I had worked in, I lost no time in getting down to work - but this was a somewhat larger area and responsibility than I had experienced before; there was a huge in-tray demanding my attention. Every day new issues would hit my desk. On my first day, I visited Bishop Bell School – now called St. Catherine's College - the large Church of England secondary school in the Langney area of Eastbourne, opened by H.R.H. Princess Margaret in 1958 and dedicated by Bishop Bell. This was his last act after twenty-nine years as bishop, and he was to die shortly afterwards. He had specifically requested that the school be built in a less affluent and expanding area of Eastbourne. Whenever I entered that building, which also housed his mitre and crozier, I never felt that this courageous and truly great bishop was far away.

The rural dean was expected to serve as chair of governors of the school, the 1986 Education Act having increased the responsibilities of all governing bodies. The school had passed through a difficult period, and was taking time to recover. The challenges were many: adopting to new technology; responding to the demands of the new education acts; and coping with a more competitive approach among schools. The diocese and deanery tried hard to raise the profile of the school, but with little success.

While I always enjoyed my times in the school and being with pupils and staff, I realised that I could not give the time that was now required of chairs of governors - and after three years handed over to Fr. John Ashby, Vicar of St. Mary's, Willingdon, himself a teacher. After two years he found it too much, so I asked one of the other governors, John Godby, who had extensive experience in management, if he would take it on 'for about a year'. In the event, he remained in office for nearly twenty years. The significant change for which we had all been praying came in 1995 with the appointment of Terry Boatwright as head teacher. In under four years, Bishop Bell School became one of the most improved schools in the country. A few years later it was oversubscribed.

Terry is a man rich in faith and full of the Holy Spirit. He did not believe in indoctrination, but in living out the principles of the Christian Faith. So I was pleased to introduce him to my old friend and new colleague, the former Bishop of Aston in Birmingham Diocese, Bishop Mark Green - who soon became a voluntary part-time chaplain to the school. Mark (then in his late seventies) was quite a shy man, but possessed an astonishing gift for relating to young people, and helping them to see how exciting the Christian Faith can be. The Eucharists he celebrated in school for year groups were deeply inspiring and you could hear the proverbial pin drop. I was privileged to return to the school as Bishop of Blackburn to be the principal guest at the Awards Evening in 2005. Bishop Mark sat in the front row, and I was conscious that this inspirational former army chaplain - who was decorated for his gallantry in rescuing wounded soldiers in the heat of battle - would have had something more exciting and perceptive to say to young people. But he had the humility never to make comparisons, and always gave encouragement. It has been a joy to return to the school in retirement and above all to be present on the evening when Terry Boatwright left after eighteen years of service to the school.

There were many challenges in the parish. I knew my predecessor, Canon Cyril Bess, as we were rural deans together in the same archdeaconry. He was a most able and dedicated parish priest and had built up a good congregation at St. Mary's. There was need for some new thinking and a number of changes, but very broadly the job would be one of continuation and consolidation. Cyril and his wife, Eunice, had retired into the east of the town, and never tried to interfere, and when he died I was invited to celebrate his Funeral Mass. A short while later, his wife graciously asked if I would object if she moved back into the parish, which she did and was never anything other than supportive.

Canon Bess had quite a good stewardship scheme in place, which we built upon. We had to work very hard for our income, but were fortunate in receiving occasional small legacies from the congregation. I was blessed with the finest of treasurers, Brian Etheridge, a chartered accountant in the town. Indeed, I was fortunate in having excellent lay officers throughout the nearly ten years I spent in Eastbourne; this was helped along by some good social occasions, and people with a keen sense of humour - none more so than one of the wardens, Commodore Derek Patterson, to whom everyone was 'old boy'. Seldom have I ever encountered anyone able to laugh at himself to the same degree.

The church and other buildings were maintained to a high standard; but having three of the oldest buildings in Eastbourne - one the size of a small cathedral - meant, like the Forth Bridge, that there was constant maintenance. Among the building projects was the very costly restoration of the Old Parsonage Barn, adjacent to the Old Parsonage, with facilities for meetings, teaching and social outreach; the construction in the church cloister of one of the most expensive lavatories in the Church of England (to blend in with a Grade 1 listed building); and the replacing of the organ. The generosity of a far-from-wealthy congregation ensured that the money was always found for whatever we needed to undertake.

Following the elections to diocesan boards, councils and committees, just after I arrived, I was now on the Bishop's Council and the Diocesan Board of Finance, the Diocesan Pastoral Committee, and the bishop, from time to time, put me on *ad hoc* committees and asked me to undertake various tasks.

As Vicar of St. Mary's, I was careful not to hand over all the pastoral work to the deputy vicar and curate and just focus on the work outside the parish – that would have made me an 'absentee parish priest'. As the outside work increased, life became very full, so I had to look at my priorities. It would have been wrong to reduce my daily devotional commitments, because adoration of God the Holy Trinity, the Mass and the Office, constitute our principal responsibility and certainly our first calling as priests - it is what we are here for. With the ever-increasing tasks before me I needed to find a finer balance. I learnt also to delegate effectively, and to work far more with and through lay people.

In my first December, the diocesan bishop invited me to represent his staff (of which, of course, I was not a member) at Launde Abbey, where a conference had been arranged for some twenty-five Evangelical clergy who were now ministering in parishes of other traditions - some in fairly advanced Catholic ones. The conference was facilitated by a priest who was in such a parish, Canon Graham Dow, Vicar of Holy Trinity Coventry; he later became my 'neighbour' and friend when I went to Blackburn, and he was Bishop of Carlisle. I found the clergy easy to relate to and we had much common ground; I was confident that some bridges could be built between us. I was heartened when a straw poll was taken and all but three said that their vocation and ministry had been enriched by their new situation, and that they would not request a return to an established evangelical parish.

Above all, this conference was a bold sign to me that, as Catholics of whatever shade, we had a real problem if some traditional Catholic parishes were now being run by those trained in the Evangelical tradition. It seemed inevitable that many of our parishes would become Liberal Evangelical, albeit with a more important place accorded to the Eucharist by them. Indeed, the first National Evangelical Congress - which took place at Keele University in 1967 and established a new agenda for Evangelical Anglicans - had committed delegates to working towards a weekly communion as the central corporate service of the Church.

At the second conference, in 1977, Prebendary John Stott from All Souls', Langham Place made another most hopeful statement when he said, 'The Church is and must be defined sacramentally by Baptism... we could do worse than use it as a definition of the Church.' For sure, the Evangelicals were building bridges, and it is therefore little wonder that they are now so generously represented in the College of Bishops and currently occupy four out of five of the most senior bishoprics.

Shortly after this conference, the Bishop invited me to chair a working party on liturgy and music with his chaplain, Fr. Jeremy Haselock, a liturgist, as secretary. This marked the start of a good working relationship over a number of years; out of the Liturgy and Music Working Party came the Diocesan Liturgical Committee, which I was also asked to chair. By now the *Alternative Service Book* (1980) was well established; supplementary material for Lent, Holy Week and Easter, and the period from All Saints to Candlemas had also been published. In 1991, I chose to write about and make a presentation on this supplementary material when I attended a mid-service course for clergy at St. George's, Windsor Castle

Not long after the Windsor Course, I had a month's study leave - part of it spent at St. Stephen's House - when I wrote a small booklet on the subject of concelebration of the Eucharist. Before the ordination of women to the priesthood, I could not understand why there was all the huffing and puffing about concelebration. If the ministerial priesthood is essentially a shared ministry - shared primarily with the Lord, and then also with the bishop and other priests – concelebration is an expression of this.

The service for the ordination of priests in the Church of England, and the declaration a priest makes before taking up an appointment, reinforces this when it speaks of the setting apart of a person by and for Christ in His Church. Whatever some people might believe about ordination, the Church is clear that it is more than the commissioning of someone to exercise certain functions in the Church as pastoral need requires. Rather, ordination is the setting apart of a man by and for Christ in His Church, 'so that he lives what he is'; and concelebration emphasises this. (The Church of England, of course, also now accepts that it is possible for a woman to do this, although a significant minority of us find this break unacceptable, because we share the traditional three-fold ministry of Bishops, Priests and Deacon, with other churches - most notably the

Roman Catholic Church and the Orthodox Church of the East. Such a decision we do not believe can be made unilaterally.)

It also seems extraordinary that a church which is trying to build up collaborative working among the clergy, wanted to revert to seeing the priest as a solo performer at public worship. We can be very inconsistent. I have always encouraged concelebration, even after the ordination of women to the priesthood - providing no priest was discriminated against and no one was being asked to act against their conscience.

St. Mary's Eastbourne was a notch 'down-the-candle' compared with my previous incumbencies; but this presented no problem to me, because I am not into old-fashioned high-church ceremonial. So long as I did not introduce incense, there seemed to be no issues. There were some changes, however, that we needed to make, to be a little closer to the spirit of the 'post-conciliar Church' – and, indeed, to the way the Church of England itself was evolving at that time. Consequently, we introduced concelebration, with sometimes as many as five or six priests concelebrating at the Parish Eucharist (we had a staff of eight priests, four of whom were retired). With the paschal liturgy for the three solemn days in Holy Week, the parish was half-way there; it was a small step to introduce a full Holy Week, including an excellent Easter Vigil, with over one hundred communicants (it lasted only one-and-a-quarter hours with a good party afterwards). Interestingly, the Vigil did not seem to affect attendances at the Easter morning Masses. At the same time, we introduced a Holy Hour before the Blessed Sacrament each week.

While St. Mary's was not a 'five star' Anglo-Catholic parish, I recognised among the people there a commitment and discipline to the faith and worship of the Church Catholic that is not always evident in many more advanced parishes. That was just one reason that it was such a fine training ground for curates, and all of mine went on to responsible posts. The curates exercised a wide and full ministry in the parish, and I ensured that they had the opportunity to minister in the deanery as well. Two of them, Fr. Martin Onions and Fr. Kevin Agnew, had exceptional gifts for working with children, young people and their families. Soon after he arrived in the summer of 1988, Martin formed Noah's Ark – a twenty-minute afternoon service for babies and toddlers. Afterwards they adjourned to the Old Parsonage Hall for projects and activities and refreshments, before parents went to collect other children from school.

Noah's Ark was enthusiastically received; I felt it was right to offer a non-eucharistic service during the week. Previously, I had always taken the view that the Family Service was the Mass – which it is – but there are other valid means of coming to know the Lord. Fr. Martin - who later became one of my best friends - died very suddenly aged fifty-one while Vicar and Rural Dean of Uckfield. In the address at his Requiem Mass in June 2014, I said that Noah's Ark (which is still running) was the forerunner of today's increasingly popular 'Messy Church'.

We did not see Noah's Ark as 'alternative church' but, rather, as both an explorers' group and a stepping-stone into the Family Service, and the Parish Eucharist, and Junior Church. An encouraging number of parents sought confirmation. We were fortunate, also, in Fr. Kevin Agnew, who came to me towards the end of my incumbency and led the parish through the vacancy. Kevin's workshops for children at half terms, in Holy Week and during summer holidays, were heavily subscribed, and introduced many to the church. These were also enjoyed by young people of our own congregation. It was pleasing that St. Mary's was increasingly being seen as a very 'child-friendly' church.

During my time in Eastbourne, we were richly blessed in having Neil Parsons – a recent music graduate - as Director of Music; he was followed by David Kemp, a secondary-school teacher. Both gave most generously of their time to the choir, to the musical life of the church, and, particularly, to the junior choir. They encouraged young people with their Royal School of Church Music medals awards, choir camps and outings were organised. Each year the whole choir sang the services in a cathedral for a week. Long-lasting friendships were established among members of the junior choir. A number of them continue to sing in choirs, one is now director of music at a major parish church in the North, and three have become priests.

One of the great blessings of being in Eastbourne was to have as my confessor and spiritual director the Vicar of St Saviour's, Canon Derek Allen, a former Principal of the Anglo-Catholic Theological College, St. Stephen's House. To be taking on such a tremendous task with this wise and holy priest close by was an encouragement. He had a gift for listening, and in the most gentle and loving way seemed to know his penitents at the deepest level. He also had the great gift of plumbing the depths of what I had been saying – often at considerable length - and then dropping in an absolute pearl of wisdom, or a quotation from St. Francis de Sales, often, too, referring me to helpful reading.

The day before his sudden death, I had travelled with him to St. Paul's Cathedral on the train. We had to change at Haywards Heath, and, as we had a thirty-minute wait, I suggested coffee and a croissant. True to form, Derek, who had turned hesitancy into an art, responded in his familiar way with 'Should we, Nicholas?' As we waited for our connection on the platform, he dropped one of those pearls of wisdom which opened so many doors for me – the last of the many gifts he gave to me.

As rural dean, I was responsible for organising Derek's Funeral Mass. Ninety-nine priests asked to concelebrate, and, in addition, eight bishops attended, including the Bishop of London. Predictably, there was standing room only. The Dean of Exeter, Richard Eyre, preached the sermon, 'A Singular and Precious

Being', which was later privately printed in Fr. Peter Cobb's memoir, *Derek William Allen* (1992). The book also contains a number of Derek's sermons and writings.

Organising the service was quite simple in comparison with clearing out Derek's study - and there was also the challenge represented by Miki, Fr. Derek's undisciplined cat. Now quite old, and needing some expensive medicine, I was confident the vet would call time. Instead he sent a message through to say, 'Canon Allen's cat is quite healthy and has a few more years in him.' No one wanted him, apart from our daughter, Claire. In a moment of weakness on a very snowy day, I went down to St. Saviour's Vicarage to fetch Miki. Needless to say, our resident cat, Peter, was far from happy. Two-and-a-half years later, when Miki died, I told Bishop Eric Kemp that Derek's cat had died, expecting him to be rather sad. His response was 'that must be a relief'. It was - but he was such a character, and like his previous owner, mischievous.

The previous year we had an even larger Funeral Mass at St. Saviour's. From the moment I arrived in Eastbourne, both Christine and I warmed to the local Member of Parliament, Ian Gow, and to his wife, Jane. Ian had been an Opposition spokesman on Northern Ireland, then, in 1979, when the Conservatives came into government he became Parliamentary Private Secretary to Mrs Thatcher for four years. He was then Minister of State for Housing for two-and-a-half years. His last post in Government was as Minister of State at the Treasury, from which he resigned. Always a man of principle, he had concerns over the direction of the Government's policy on Northern Ireland.

Ian was an outstanding constituency MP, and whoever needed his help received it. He seemed to be in the constituency nearly all the time, and I only remember him going on holiday once – to Jersey for four days. Ian was also a committed Anglo-Catholic, and cared greatly about the work of the church in the deanery. He became the first (and, for a while, the only) churchwarden at St. Luke's Church, Stone Cross, which re-opened some three months after we arrived in Eastbourne; and a very charismatic priest was appointed, who became a great friend of Ian and Jane. After the re-dedication of the church, in June 1988, we went for lunch at the Gows' home. That was the first of many visits we enjoyed at 'The Dog House'. We always had both serious conversation there and huge fun. If we visited at the weekend, a cabinet minister or other prominent parliamentarian would invariably be a fellow guest.

Every year since its inception, I had taken part in the Sussex Historic Churches Trust Sponsored Bicycle Ride, usually riding a tandem. The first tandem I rode (while at Mayfield) was two old Post Office bikes welded together and built by the curate of St. Peter's Bexhill. Unfortunately, half-a-mile out of Mayfield, they parted. In 1988, Ian Gow agreed to ride a sturdier tandem with me around the Eastbourne deanery; and, when we stopped at The Dog House for lunch, he insisted on riding two laps of honour around the edge of his swimming pool.

Tragically, Ian was assassinated by a bomb placed under his car by IRA terrorists in late July 1990, twelve years after his friend and fellow shadow Northern Ireland Minister, Airey Neve, was murdered in a similar way. Christine and I received the news while we were on holiday in Guernsey - we were due to return the next day and then, four days later, to set off with a party from the parish to Oberammergau. I did what I could in the limited time available to plan the funeral, and then flew back from Zurich for the service.

1988: Eastbourne Parish Church. Setting off on a tandem with Ian Gow, MP, on a Sussex Historic Churches Trust sponsored Bicycle Ride.

The Prime Minister and many of her cabinet attended the Funeral Mass, which the diocesan bishop celebrated, with the Bishop of Lewes preaching. The streets were lined with people wanting to pay their respects to a courageous and respected MP who had cared for them. I went with the priest from Stone Cross to The Dog House for tea with the family, close friends and various politicians - meeting several whom I had only ever seen on television. I also spoke to Mrs Thatcher and her daughter, whom Ian once brought to the vicarage when he was showing her the sights of Eastbourne. I had my glass refilled while talking to Denis Thatcher. The Thatchers left early, and everyone waved dutifully as a helicopter scooped them away. This was the time of the beginning of the Gulf War, and, from the conversations going on after the Prime Minister left, it was rather obvious there was some tension around. Margaret Thatcher only remained Prime Minister for some four months after that.

We had let a family from a previous parish stay in the vicarage while we were in Oberammergau, so I was glad, on my brief return to Eastbourne, to stay with Fr. Jeffrey Williams, then our recently-arrived new curate. Jeff had come to me with degrees in English and Theology, and a Diploma in Drama; he had also been on the Bishop of Lewes' scheme for young people, before going to Chichester Theological College. It was clear to me that his potential was not realised at the seminary - so it was a particular joy to see him in the parish opening up like a flower. He had a gift for contemplative prayer, and was a very thoughtful and engaging preacher, with rare pastoral gifts. Jeff was artistic, and good at dealing with conflict, with a wonderful sense of humour - he was truly brilliant at 'sending me up'. Early on, he showed real signs of promise, and after four years with us he went to St. John's, Upper St. Leonards for twelve years, where a real transformation took place in the parish. I was honoured to preach at St. Mary's, Twickenham for the Silver Jubilee of his priesting, in 2016. While not reducing his commitment to living and teaching the Catholic way of life, he has also developed a most impressive civic ministry. He was a prayerful supporter during my Blackburn years, and it is a joy to meet up with him from time to time.

I was fortunate in having fine curates in Eastbourne, and I enjoyed the company of all of them. They all went on to posts in which their ministry and gifts could flourish. One, Fr. John Lees (a gifted musician and administrator), became a Minor Canon and Succentor at St. Paul's Cathedral, London. I was also fortunate in having a number of retired priests to assist, all of whom enriched the life of the parish. I have already referred to Bishop Mark Green's ministry among young people. We were blessed indeed to have him in Eastbourne - particularly so soon after the loss of Canon Derek Allen, another wise, experienced and highly-regarded spiritual director and confessor. We much appreciated Mark's special addresses at Lent, and his regular sermons at the Parish Mass and Choral Evensong; they had rare insight but were easy to listen to.

Mark was one of the best communicators I came across in my ministry. I will never forget his sermon at the Drumhead Service on Eastbourne seafront, in 1994, to celebrate the fiftieth anniversary of the Dunkirk landing. Throughout the address he held the huge crowd spellbound, particularly as he spoke in the most natural way about meeting God in the horror of that day, and how God is nearest when suffering is greatest. Mark had an extensive ministry among ex-Service personnel in the town, and to this day is still remembered and widely missed. In his last book, *Before I Go* (2005), Mark writes about his spiritual journey, and includes a diary of part of his active service at the time of the D Day landings, and sermons from his retirement ministry.

There was nothing cheap in Mark's life. He was able to give so generously to us at St. Mary's and elsewhere, because he had been up against many struggles in life. I admired Bishop Mark and benefitted greatly from his wisdom, rejoicing to have him as a colleague and a close friend – he was someone with whom I could share much. For the twenty-fifth anniversary of his ordination and consecration as Bishop, the parish gave him a silver pectoral cross. I was deeply touched that he left it to me, and also that I have the crozier that was given him to him at his consecration, which I carry at special services from time to time.

Christine continued to teach part-time at the convent school at Mayfield; after four terms at Meads Church of England School, Claire became a weekly boarder at the convent. Christine was sometimes asked by the convent if she would have boarders who were experiencing some pastoral difficulty to stay for a weekend - or even longer. At the end of the academic year all of Christine's students who were leaving came down in a minibus for a celebration - and as they were over eighteen years of age we brought out a little wine. On one occasion, something must have gone wrong for a girl was ill the following morning and went to the doctor (who was also a friend of ours). The doctor tried to find out what the problem was; eventually he asked where she had been the night before and what she had drunk. 'Oh goodness', he said, 'I know what's wrong with you', and it is alleged he wrote in her notes 'Went down to the Reades' and came back in the usual state'.

In addition to her Mayfield teaching commitment, Christine also taught 'A' level Religious Studies for three years at Beresford House Girls' School, around the corner from the vicarage. One of her two students there went on be ordained, and later became Vice-Principal of Westcott House Theological College in Cambridge.

Christine was very good at ensuring that we took holidays. We tried to take a week after Christmas and Easter - often visiting family - but most summers we spent three weeks in the Channel Islands, generally in Guernsey. Claire would spend hours in the sea on her surf board, but when she reached the age of about fourteen she preferred to stay with friends from school who lived in more exciting places like Malta and Los Angeles. Of her own free will, Claire decided to follow in the footsteps of her parents and grandfather by going to Leeds University to read Theology with English - her first year being spent in the same hall of residence that Christine had lived in, many years earlier.

I still have on my desk the cannon given to me by Claire on the day that I became a Canon of the Cathedral and Prebendary of Marden. The archdeacon told me that the bishop usually made the Vicar of Eastbourne a Canon on his appointment, but I had to wait a while as I was younger than my predecessors. I was pleased that I did not have to wait too long, as that was the only one of my last three senior appointments that came before my mother died. It was a beautiful summer's evening, and, on the way back from Chichester Cathedral, we stopped for a picnic supper, overlooking Arundel Castle as the sun went down. I enjoyed my greater involvement with the cathedral and, following the passing of the Cathedrals Measure (1999), which made significant changes to the governance of a cathedral, I was pleased to serve on the transitional council, which was created 'to frame with the consent of the bishop, instruments providing for the constitution and statutes of the cathedral'.

Mention has already been made of how much the ordination of women to the priesthood debate sapped the energy of the Church of England over many years. It was in November 1992 when the General Synod narrowly gave the proposed Measure the requisite two-thirds majority in all three Houses – Bishops, Clergy and Laity. Of course, this was not an issue about the equality of women or whether women would be 'up to the job'. How many times did we hear it said, that we have had a woman Prime Minister with real guts, surely, we can have women priests? The argument is about something very different, for it is to do with the world of sacramental signs.

For me, the main arguments against the ordination of women were to do with the nature of the Church Catholic and the claim of the Church of England that its ordained ministry is recognisably that of the whole Catholic Church (East and West). Accordingly, a major change in the sacrament of holy order could not be made by just one small section of the Church. There is a choice for us: to be a part of the One Holy Catholic and Apostolic Church, or just one Protestant sect among many.

Conservative evangelicals in the Church joined many Catholic Anglicans in not supporting the proposed legislation, but on the grounds of headship: God is the God of order and has created all things for our good. They argue from sacred scripture that God has appointed men to be head of the family. When applied to headship in the church, the order of creation consequently does not permit women to be priests or bishops. I have some sympathy with this argument, but I cannot fully endorse it; however, it was worthy of greater respect and consideration in the debate than I believe it received. There is a strong argument related to this approach: I always will believe that as God sent His Son 'in the fullness of time' there must be a finality about the revelation of the God-Man, Jesus Christ, which cannot be changed.

Notwithstanding this, if the whole Church (East and West) declared that to ordain women would simply represent a development of the received tradition and not a change, I would accept that without question. As it was, when I became a bishop, I could not ordain women to the priesthood, because, as a bishop of the Church Catholic, I did not believe I had the authority to do so. However, I permitted one of my suffragans to do so, and all women priests held my licence and I instituted them to parishes. I acknowledge the inconsistency in my approach, but I was always mindful that the bishop is the sign of unity in his diocese, and should exercise a real ministry of encouragement to all who hold his licence.

The days after the decision in 1992 were very difficult in the Eastbourne deanery, with so many clergy, both Catholic and Evangelical, opposed to the decision - some truly wondered about their future. I visited them in their homes and tried to 'steady the ship'. There was some uncertainty about the provision that would be made for those of us who were keen to remain in the Church of England. I was confident that the House of Bishops would make provision for us - which, eventually, they did, with the Episcopal Ministry Act of Synod (1993). This ensured that those of our integrity would not be asked to do anything that would be against our conscience in the new dispensation. I always remember Bishop Eric Kemp's words, when he gathered us all together in All Saints' Hove a couple of weeks after the vote; he quoted St. Jerome (342-420) writing after the Church made another decision against the received tradition:

> 'We woke up and the whole world groaned and was astonished to find itself Arian..... the ship of the Apostles was in peril, she was driven by the wind. Her sides were beaten with the waves; no hope was now left.'

The bishop went on remind us that some hundred years afterwards, the situation had been resolved and orthodoxy restored.

While a number of priests left the diocese - mostly for the Roman Catholic Communion - only one left in the Eastbourne deanery. These were difficult days, and I was to have more difficult days after I became Bishop of Blackburn, when the Church of England prepared, and eventually passed, legislation to enable women to become bishops. In the second year of my episcopate, I was asked to join the Guildford Group, under the chairmanship of Christopher Hill (Bishop of Guildford) to develop a proposal to put before the Synod.

There were five of us in the group, and I was the only traditionalist, but we worked together harmoniously. The group came up with a proposal for Transferred Episcopal Arrangements (TEA). It was rather difficult to convince some of my colleagues that the transferred arrangements must not only apply when the diocesan bishop was a woman, but whenever the diocesan bishop was party to consecrating women. At the General Synod, in February that year, every member - save one (who was from Blackburn Diocese) - voted to take TEA forward; but following a review by a very small, and unrepresentative group, when we returned for the July Synod, it was decided to pull the plug on TEA.

It was a long haul to find an alternative solution that would enable women priests to be raised to the episcopate, and it did not arrive until 2013. I am pleased to admit that the final decision, when the Synod welcomed the House of Bishops 'Declaration on the Ministry of Bishops and Priests' and the 'Five Guiding Principles', was far more satisfactory than TEA. I believe we now have something in place that is workable, even if not quite the solution many of us would have wanted to see.

My life on the General Synod did not actually begin until 1995, when I was elected by the clergy of the diocese; later, I became the representative archdeacon. My synod number, which you have to declare whenever you stand up to speak, was never difficult to remember: 123. I recall making my maiden speech on an amendment from the Chichester Diocesan Synod relating to a crisis in the farming community, in which I called for a retirement scheme for tenant farmers and for financial help for organisations supporting rural families.

When Bishop Ian Cundy became the Area Bishop of Lewes in 1992, he was keen to introduce a more strategic way of working. He wished to focus more on the deanery unit and to provide training for the clergy in collaborative ministry. He was also anxious to ensure that we took seriously the Decade of Evangelism, and later on was pleased to hear of the possibility of a deanery mission somewhere in his area.

When I arrived in Eastbourne, I looked at possible ways to encourage parishes to work together - I think with a measure of success. One morning I received a phone call from Martin Cavender from 'Springboard' - which was an initiative of the two archbishops to further the work of evangelism in the course of the decade. He said that they would like to have a deanery mission within one of the Springboard courses, and that they wanted it to be in Eastbourne. It immediately occurred to me that God the Holy Spirit must have been hard at work.

The leaders of 'Springboard' were Bishop Michael Marshall, a former Bishop of Woolwich, and Dr. Michael Green (1930-2019), a well-known Evangelical, who had once been Principal of St. John's College, Nottingham. Michael Green came to meet the deanery clergy, and I clicked with him immediately - he was a joy to work with. He told us that the School of Evangelism would last two weeks, with one of the participants on the course assigned to each parish. Every parish would be responsible for running its own mission and could use the assigned evangelist in any way they wished. There were to be 'warm up' events in the deanery during the six months preceding the mission. I remember Bishop Mark Green, now some few years into his time with me, taking a prominent part in these activities. During the intensive mission fortnight there would also be deanery 'umbrella events'. It was thrilling to have the whole deanery engaging in mostly different mission activities, and also joining together in the corporate events.

I really cannot doubt that the Holy Spirit was very much at work in the deanery during that time. As always, it is difficult to evaluate what came out of the mission. The Spirit always works for unity and towards charity. Afterwards, we were for the most part better at working together. Certainly, some came to a more personal devotion to the Lord. Many in our congregations who were previously uncomfortable about sharing their faith found a new confidence in talking about their journey. I must admit that the follow-up activities were less successful. Parishes with Alpha and other existing evangelistic nurture groups were well-equipped for this, but they were in the minority. I had hoped to facilitate this work, but, not too long afterwards, Bishop Eric came to talk to me about deanery matters, and, at the end just dropped the question, 'Would you like to think about becoming Archdeacon of Lewes and Hastings?'

8 MUCH MORE THAN DRAINS AND DOWNPIPES. ARCHDEACON OF LEWES AND HASTINGS

Before we moved to Lewes, Christine had never liked the town; but almost immediately we moved there she loved it. While both of us missed belonging to a parish after twenty-four years, we rather liked the comparative anonymity. We had a house with a number, and there were no unwanted callers. We very much liked the house (27 The Avenue) as had my predecessor, Archdeacon Hugh Glaisyer. Somebody told us, 'Anyone who is anybody lives in The Avenue' – but as it turned out, there was little consciousness of social status in Lewes.

As archdeacon, I was responsible under the bishop for one hundred and eighty-eight churches in the archdeaconry, but I did not have 'my own' church. The parish priest of St. Michael's invited me to celebrate the eight o'clock Mass every Friday morning, and several of my regular church commitments in the diocese and archdeaconry began with Mass. I was always in a parish for the Eucharist on Sundays, and - although I was not the bishop – twenty-nine times out of thirty the parish clergy invited me to celebrate the Eucharist: so I was hardly starved of Eucharistic worship or presidency of the Mass. We set aside an oratory in the house for the daily offices and other prayer, and the diocesan bishop gave me permission to reserve the Blessed Sacrament - that also enabled me to take the Blessed Sacrament to clergy who were sick.

I asked Bishop Eric how he would like me to fulfil the post. His reply was, 'with a little less enthusiasm'. The bishop greatly respected Hugh, my predecessor, who was 'on top of everything'. Eric was pastoral, scholarly, and a good administrator, but he came from more relaxed times, and suspected that the clergy liked an efficient, caring, but fairly relaxed, approach. I did say to the bishop that I could not do the job as some kind of priestly administrator: I wanted to be 'a pastoral archdeacon'. He was happy with that. Indeed, the happiest time of the week was getting behind the wheel on a Sunday morning and going to a parish - usually for the Eucharist, and invariably to preach. I preached or celebrated (and often both) in all 188 churches in the archdeaconry - several times in many of them.

When the bishop had come to see me in Eastbourne, he was very open, and said that he and the Archbishops' Appointments Adviser felt I would be more suited to being a suffragan bishop. But they wanted me to have this post, and I was not to see it as a consolation prize. There was a real job to be done, and I would be working with a new Bishop of Lewes - an Irishman, Wallace Benn, about the same age as me - who had been Vicar of Harold Wood in the Diocese of Chelmsford. He was a convinced Evangelical and a member of the Reform Group. Eric, who was usually right about things, said that I would get on well with him, in spite of some of our theological differences. How right he proved to be.

The archdeacon can be seen as a 'number two' in the

diocesan hierarchy. The function is much to do with the temporalities, and is, perhaps, best represented in the service of institution of a priest. At the beginning of a new ministry, the priest is given spiritual authority to minister in the parish by the bishop. The powerful symbol of this is the giving of the deed of institution and the Bishop's words 'receive the cure of souls which is both yours and mine in the name of the Father, and of the Son, and of the Holy Spirit.' After that, the archdeacon inducts the priest into the corporal possession of the benefice, because the archdeacon has responsibility for the temporalities of the Church. Much of the archdeacon's time is taken up with the care of church buildings, including parsonage houses, and helping parishes to make their submission to the church's planning authority (the Diocesan Advisory Council for the Care of Churches). The archdeacon also serves on, and chairs, numerous diocesan boards, councils and committees, and is the 'chief trouble-shooter'. Chichester Diocese has a large number of church schools – although nothing like the number in Blackburn Diocese. I enjoyed that involvement, especially when I could take school assemblies or talk to classes of children.

Every archdeacon has some responsibilities outside the archdeaconry. The bishop asked me to be Bishop's Adviser for Hospital Chaplaincy, which involved visiting the hospitals in East and West Sussex with their chaplains, interviewing prospective chaplains, and taking up any issues of concern with the hospital management. I also represented the chaplains on the bishop's staff. I had always felt a strong pull to hospital work, giving priority to visiting parishioners – with the fondest memories of my time in Dudley as a part-time chaplain.

I was also asked to be Chair of the Readers' Committee. Given all the work that readers do, the title 'reader' is very misleading – indeed, some dioceses now call them 'lay ministers'. Their training is extensive and covers much of the same ground as those who are preparing for ordained ministry. I was privileged to work with two gifted Bishop's Advisers for Lay Ministry. Dr. John Mantle went on to be the Bishops' Training Officer at Church House, Westminster, and played an important part in preparing me for episcopal ministry. Later he became Bishop of Brechin in the Scottish Episcopal Church, and, sadly, died after five years in the post, aged only sixty-four. Joy Gilliver, who succeeded John in that post, was gifted with a deep Catholic understanding of the Church, had good ideas for lay training, and an ability to translate that into practice. After thirteen years, she was made redundant, and I was delighted that the Ministry Division of the Archbishops' Council appointed her as one of their Selection Secretaries, a post for which she was well qualified.

Joy is a 'traditionalist' in the Church of England, and, also, like me, and more than ninety percent of the traditionalists in the Church of England, she is keen to work on good terms with everyone in the Church. It has to be said that we have not always felt that the liberal majority in the Church have returned the compliment, and, over the years, few of our persuasion have held key positions in the Ministry Division. Joy's appointment restored much of my faith in the fairness of the system; she has also demonstrated that those who cannot accept the ordination of women on grounds of conscience also respect the position of those who hold a different view. We can work across the whole church and be involved in the selection of women for training for the priesthood.

It was a privilege to work with two Wardens of Readers, the second of these was Canon Peter Atkinson, the last Principal of Chichester Theological College, and, later, Dean of Worcester. In my judgement he is one of the finest preachers in the Church. However, my greatest joy was working with the readers themselves. They exercise a sterling ministry in the parishes - not just leading non-eucharistic services, preaching and teaching, but also fulfilling a significant pastoral and evangelistic role. I have been particularly impressed by the disciplined devotional lives that many of them lead. When I was at Blackburn we were honoured to host the National Readers' Conference, at the University of Lancaster. At the Conference Eucharist, a reader, Jean Pearson (the wife of the Suffragan Bishop of Lancaster), preached the sermon - in her whole ministry and service in the Church she epitomised the strength of the reader ministry.

As archdeacon, I often drove in excess of five hundred miles a week. Unlike in Lancashire, the road network was not good, with only a few miles of dual carriageway in East Sussex. I became used to reciting one of the Daily Offices while parked in my car and also to taking my 'Action Man' lunch box with me. If possible, and within the budget, I would take clergy out for a simple lunch - if that was appropriate for the business we needed to do. I endorse the emphasis that the religious communities place upon the ministry of hospitality and entertainment. At home in Lewes, Christine and I enjoyed entertaining large numbers of people, including rural deans and lay chairs and as many of the clergy as possible.

Working relationships with the Diocesan Secretary (called in some dioceses 'the chief executive') were very good, as with the Chair of the Diocesan Advisory Council for the Care of Churches, John Ebdon. Nothing was ever too much trouble for John, even my nine o'clock call most Sunday evenings. I particularly enjoyed working with my fellow Archdeacons - of Chichester and of Horsham – Michael Brotherton and William Filby, to begin with, and then Douglas McKittrick and Roger Combes. The eight rural deans in the archdeaconry were my team, and they would also undertake some of the archdeacon's triennial visitations. Church House, Hove, practically became a second home. I had always had the highest regard for Eric Kemp, the diocesan bishop, who, remarkably, was over eighty years old at the time of my appointment. He was deeply prayerful and insightful, a leading authority on canon law, a respected scholar, and always balanced. Although he was famously shy, he could be very good company, and had a wonderful sense of humour - there was much laughter at bishop's staff meetings. I was greatly honoured to speak at the farewell dinner for Bishop Eric given by his General Synod representatives, and remember referring to his correspondence on liturgical matters with my late father-in-law.

Eric was succeeded by Bishop John Hind (Bishop of Gibraltar in Europe), whom Christine had known at University, and I had come to know, successively, as Principal of Chichester Theological College, and as Bishop of Horsham. I warmed to John's understanding of the nature of the Church, and found him easy to talk to. When I became a diocesan bishop, I came to appreciate him even more. In the House of Bishops he was much respected as one of the few with a fine theological mind - even though he did not pull any punches. From him, I found a greater confidence to speak in that august gathering, although my style was perhaps more eirenic than his. At my farewell Eucharist, given by the archdeaconry at St. Saviour's Eastbourne, I said, from the heart, that if I were to do anything good as Bishop of Blackburn, much of it would be down to what I had seen and learnt from Bishop Eric and Bishop John; they, with some others, had shown me by example what it is to be a faithful overseer and guardian of the faith; a leader in mission and servant of the Church; and, above all, chief minister of word and sacrament.

At that final service, I recall making something of

the fact that St. Francis de Sales (whose memorial fell on that day) was working in Geneva at the same time as the reformer, John Calvin. The bishop with whom I had worked most closely in the archdeaconry, was, of course, the Bishop of Lewes (who had been consecrated on the same day that Tony Blair became Prime Minister): therefore he and I started our work together. Wallace was a great devotee of John Calvin, but we both believed in a revealed faith: that the Gospel is truth and must be shared and spread. Everything else is to be seen in the light of that conviction. The partnership between the area bishop and archdeacon worked well, and our wives were good friends too.

I am grateful that Bishop Wallace shared so much with me, and gave me a great deal of responsibility; this stood me in good stead when I made the jump straight from archdeacon to diocesan bishop. Wallace, being an Irishman, had the sense of humour and wealth of jokes and stories that tend to come with that. While the thought of a day's administration may not always have excited him, being a pastor to the clergy did, and he would always thank them graciously. He loved preaching and teaching, and his Lent Bible courses offered in every deanery continue to draw warm comments from those who experienced them. I have met few people with such a great heart for mission. He showed generosity to those of us who were committed Catholics; at clergy days and conferences there were always two keynote speakers, one chosen by him and one chosen by me. He and his wife, Lindsay, were most hospitable; when I was under particular pressure, there was often a gift, or the offer of a meal. After I had chaired the Vacancy-in-See Committee and been on the Crown Appointments' Committee [CAC] (as it was then), he gave us tickets to go on The London Eye, and on one occasion, took us to Ireland for the day. His generosity was not limited to his archdeacon.

Bishop Wallace held the Suffragan See of Lewes for longer than any of his predecessors. I am sorry for Wallace that issues around cases of historic child abuse from the Lewes Area dominated his final years in post. A couple of serious matters surfaced while I was archdeacon, and I believe Wallace and I responded to these according to the practice at the time. Whilst there can never be any question that abuse is always wrong - and that those who have been abused must always be our first concern - I cannot help feeling that, as time went by, there was a lot of re-writing of good practice on the run, and in many cases the Church was being judged on how it dealt with cases in the distant past by the new guidelines and regulations.

By 2011-12 Wallace was in the firing line, and it seemed to me, from Blackburn, that it was largely to do with cases that had not actually occurred on his watch. Others involved in safeguarding, including the police, were also aware of these historic cases. True sorrow, and honouring of the courage of survivors, can be the only response to any past safeguarding failings or shortcomings. Today, at the first sign of a possible safeguarding issue in the Church, other agencies and public authorities are immediately involved and we work together. With hindsight, we see how the way the Church, and many other bodies, responded to some allegations and complaints, particularly historic ones, was often unsatisfactory. It is perfectly clear that ways of responding to allegations of abuse have now improved dramatically in the Church and in secular organisations. I began to see this in my later years as archdeacon and, most certainly, in the Diocese of Blackburn. When I returned to Chichester Diocese in retirement, it was abundantly clear that their safeguarding procedures were now a model of good practice. Nevertheless, survivors had been failed in the past by the Church, not only here but around the world, for which we must all remain deeply contrite.

There is still no simple working definition of an archdeacon, although the secular equivalent would be an area manager. In part I felt that 'Errand Boy' might be nearer the truth, because there is a strong element of 'if it doesn't fit anywhere else, give it to the archdeacon' - just remember how Anthony Trollope's Bishop Proudie ended most interviews with 'Go and see the archdeacon'. A reasonable description might be 'Steward', because the archdeacon is a steward of the resources of the church. But the most accurate one is *'Oculus Episcopi'* – the eye of the bishop: the archdeacon must know the mind of the bishop; report to the bishop; and act on behalf of the bishop, as his agent.

I was invited by the bishop to join a small panel to appoint the new Chancellor of the Diocese, the chief law officer. We met in the Bishops' Room in the House of Lords - my first visit to the House. During the interviews, the bishop made it clear that he did not want to be concerned with issues such as the 'extra liturgical service' of Benediction. I was congratulated by the bishop for suggesting that the 'the purpose of Reservation of the Blessed Sacrament is for Holy Communion of the sick, but it does not preclude advantages secondary and incidental' - words written by the Mirfield theologian, Fr. Lionel Thornton, which had suddenly come into my mind.

We appointed a most distinguished barrister, Mark Hill, who had written and lectured widely on ecclesiastical law. He worked the archdeacons hard, but was immense fun, and every year entertained the three of us to lunch at The Athenaeum. I was pleased to admit him some years later as Deputy Chancellor of Blackburn. (Unfortunately, for his commissioning, he had to sit through the dullest Diocesan Synod I can recall - he rang me later that evening to observe that the presidential address at synod had been so exciting that everyone was talking about it on the promenade at Morecambe.)

One of the toughest assignments I had in the Diocese of Chichester came after I was elected to chair the Vacancy-in-See Committee. With the resignation of Bishop Eric, at the age of eighty-six, it was widely acknowledged that the diocese needed to change - a large number even felt that this would necessitate a bishop who would himself ordain women to the priesthood. Others felt that, despite the Episcopal Ministry Act of Synod (1993), a more liberal bishop would create greater division in the diocese than a traditionalist, at this juncture. We produced for the Crown Appointments' Commission an impressive 'Statement of Needs', accurately reflecting, I believe, the current state of the diocese. Surprisingly, it contained very little on the contentious issue of the ordination of women to the priesthood - perhaps the strongest argument in favour of maintaining the *status quo* was relegated to a footnote (that the unity of the Diocese of Chichester would be best served by a bishop who would not himself ordain women).

I was pleased with the way the meetings went, and particularly with the complete absence of acrimony. I am aware of the feeling that I should take a more black-and-white approach at meetings: this was particularly the case after I became a diocesan bishop. I have always preferred the consensual way, giving as many people as possible the opportunity to express their view, and thereby to discern a way forward. Of course, the approach takes longer, and the process can be somewhat frustrating. The Prime Minister's Appointments' Secretary and the Archbishops' Appointments' Secretary both wrote after the main meeting to say 'they admired the way the meeting had been chaired'. Other members said that having a gentle hand on the tiller steering the ship to port was exactly what was needed. This was the most difficult meeting I had ever chaired, and I took that affirmation as a sign that this should always be the way to run future meetings. Truth to tell, I can never recall failing to achieve the result that I hoped for. Even at the wonderful farewell dinner to me at Blackburn given by the bishop's staff, the senior suffragan, Bishop John Goddard, said, 'we always got there in the end.'

The time of the Vacancy-in-See meetings was made additionally difficult because I received a letter inviting me to accept another post, just as the meetings reached a crucial phase. Some of those who knew me well felt I should accept the post, but deep down I believed it was not for me. After a couple of weeks - still unsure of the way forward - we came in late one night to a message on the answerphone from Bishop Mark Green. He said that I should not accept the post - it was not me. That clinched it; and immediately I was able to relax again.

Some three years later, I was working at my desk one morning when an envelope marked OHMS was delivered. Dorothy Smith, my ever-faithful secretary at that time, popped it on the desk. It was a brown envelope, so I did not bother to open it until I had a quiet moment, some two hours later. As I opened it, I noticed the Prime Minister's (Tony Blair's) signature at the bottom of a letter inviting me to become the next Bishop of Blackburn. I had been in East Sussex for twenty-two years, knew everybody and virtually every road and lane. I was fifty-six-and-a-half and had begun to think that Lewes would be my last post before retirement; although my heart lay in parish ministry, I was happy as an archdeacon because it was also a pastoral job.

How was I to respond? I have often said to clergy that if their present post is the reason for not moving on, few of us would ever move: so I decided that I had better not focus too much on what I already had. I also believed that if one receives a request to do something unexpectedly, it must be taken very seriously. I also knew that much deep prayer and thought goes into episcopal appointments, and many soundings are taken. But how could they have come up with me? What was so difficult in trying to discern if I should go to Blackburn was that the Downing Street Appointments' Adviser - for whom I had the greatest of respect - said that I could only discuss this with my spiritual director and my wife, and no one else – not even my diocesan bishop. When the announcement was eventually made, the bishop said exactly what I needed to hear, 'Nicholas, you are going back to being a parish priest.' Isn't that just what a bishop is called to be, pastor to the clergy and the whole diocese – under Jesus Christ, he is the Parish Priest?

9   INTO THE SEE – BLACKBURN (1)

The interval between receiving the invitation to become Bishop of Blackburn (from the end of June 2003 to early August), was a difficult one - not least because I had never thought of myself as a diocesan bishop. While the Church of England does not - and definitely did not, in those days - have a 'career structure', it had been mentioned that I might become a suffragan bishop one day, but no one had seriously hinted at the possibility of becoming a diocesan. Strangely, the day before I received the Prime Minister's letter, a senior member of the General Synod said to me, 'there will never be a Traditionalist Diocesan Bishop appointed again'.

I went to see Canon Michael Shields (ob. Dec. 2018), my spiritual director, and then Tony Sadler, the Archbishops' Appointments' Adviser. I also seemed to be going rather frequently through the door of No. 10 Downing Street, to see William Chapman, the Prime Minister's Appointments' Secretary, who was most helpful throughout the whole process. We worked our way through the Vacancy-in-See Committee's statement from Blackburn, and I began to see more clearly why the Crown Appointments' Commission had beaten a path to my door. I started to recognise the tune the Diocese wanted to hear, and to warm to it, but was not sure whether I could make it happen in practice. I knew I could not do it on my own, but I have often been told that one of my strengths is talent spotting, and an ability to work with people, giving them the space to see a task through. I began to think, 'maybe'. I tried never to forget that the diocese and the CAC had made the appointment a matter for sustained prayer; and I was truly amazed to learn afterwards how many people were praying for me to be the Bishop. My only priority was to be obedient to God, and, in His usual way, there were several little nudges and pointers, and I came to a positive decision.

We went to Blackburn for the announcement of my appointment - my first visit to the town. We met the Bishop's Staff, and also other key workers in the diocese. The media was out in strength. Martyn Halsall, the Bishop's Press Officer and Diocesan Communications' Officer, was helpful in preparing me for the day. Inevitably, there were questions about the wider significance of the appointment, summed up in the *Church Times* headline, 'Blackburn to retain its traditionalist stance.' I was also asked how I would deal with the British National Party, which was gaining ground in the area. I took a very firm line against the BNP, having encountered the party in its previous incarnation as the National Front when serving in Wolverhampton and Dudley; on that introductory day in Blackburn I regret not having hit them harder. However, the time for that lay ahead.

We visited Bishop's House, four miles out of Blackburn, with its stunning view over the Ribble Valley. The house was in need of considerable maintenance and improvement, much of which continued well into our first year. It was good to meet my predecessor, Bishop Alan Chesters. I had only spoken to him once before, on a sunny June afternoon ten years before; it was in the inauspicious setting of the gentlemen's lavatories at Ardingly Showground - Alan was one of the two preachers at the Chichester Diocesan Caritas jamboree. He and his wife, Jennie, soon became good friends. Our positions were similar in many areas, but our approaches were often different. I never felt anything other than support and warmth from Alan; Christine and I were deeply sorry to be out of the diocese when Jennie's Memorial Eucharist of Thanksgiving was celebrated in Blackburn Cathedral, the Archbishop of York presiding.

I was ordained and consecrated as Bishop of Blackburn on St. Chad's Day, 2 March, a special date for me, having been ordained deacon and priest in St. Chad's Cathedral, Lichfield, and having served at St. Chad's Coseley. We spent the eve of the consecration at Bishopthorpe; the Archbishop invited Claire and her fiancé, Walter, to dine with us. Also present was the other candidate for consecration, Canon James Bell, who was going to be Suffragan Bishop of Knaresborough.

I slept surprisingly well. After Matins, the archbishop blessed our episcopal rings and pectoral crosses. James Bell chose all the music for the service, and I chose the preacher, Bishop Paul Richardson, Assistant Bishop of Newcastle and previously bishop of two Australian dioceses. I was presented to the Archbishop by my present bishop, John Hind of Chichester, and the

2004. Dad in full flight at Claire and Walter's wedding.

Bishop of Lancaster, the senior suffragan in Blackburn Diocese, Stephen Pedley. The large number of co-consecrators included Bishop Eric Kemp, former Bishop of Chichester, and the Chichester suffragans, Wallace Benn and Lindsay Urwin of Horsham, to whom I also owed much; Bishop Alan Chesters, my predecessor in Blackburn; Bishop David Shepherd, former Bishop of Liverpool; the very colourful Bishop David Jenkins, formerly Bishop of Durham; and my great friend and former colleague in Eastbourne, Bishop Mark Green. I was humbled that so many had travelled such long distances from all my previous appointments to support me. As the archbishop always gives lunch to the co-consecrating bishops, we were able to have our own party for family and friends at the College of Ripon and York, St. John (now York, St. John University). Quite a number of the congregation in the cathedral thought that we had issued an open invitation - thankfully there was more than enough food and drink for everyone.

The next day, it was down to work immediately, with a morning Eucharist at 8.30 for all who work in the cathedral and at Church House, and also for the bishop's staff. This was followed by breakfast. I think it all went well. I was heartened to overhear one of the evangelical clergy saying, 'well the new Bishop celebrates like a Catholic and preaches like an Evangelical.' In the four weeks between my episcopal ordination and the installation and enthronement in the Cathedral, I endeavoured to meet as many people as possible, and gave priority in the first week to hosting an evening for the women clergy in the Diocese. All of them came; we had a buffet supper and an address, followed by a questions and answers session.

I had already made it clear that I would ordain every

deacon, but would not ordain priests, male or female, at the main Petertide ordination, confining myself to ordaining the occasional male priest who was ready for ordination outside the main season. There would be two ordinations of priests - one with the Bishop of Lancaster, and one with the Bishop of Burnley - for those candidates who requested to be ordained by a traditionalist bishop. Of course, all who were ordained would hold my licence, and I would institute every priest who came into the diocese. Every post would be open to priests of either gender, unless the Parochial Church Council had passed the 'resolutions' from the Women Priests Measure. Everyone's ministry would be valued, and was, of course, canonically valid; and everybody would be loved and cared for. When I went to parishes for the Eucharist, I wanted women priests to assist me at the Altar - but not to concelebrate - and to fulfil what is regarded as the deacon's liturgy, if there was no deacon present. I expected respect for everyone who served in the presbyterate in the diocese.

For the women priests, and many others in the Diocese, I acknowledged that it was hard to have another diocesan bishop who did not ordain women, but I was convinced that, with deep respect, love and care for each other, we could make it work. I felt this was a good meeting, and that there was real understanding between us. I hope I lived up to what I said that day. As the debate about women bishops began to ramp up, there were signs of tension; but I can honestly say that I never felt anything other than support from the women clergy, and I dare to hope that they always felt valued, respected and above all, loved, by me.

Thirteen years later, when the then Suffragan Bishop of Burnley, Philip North - one of the finest missioners in the Church and himself a traditionalist - had been chosen to be Bishop of Sheffield, it brought tears to my eyes to read the letter in the church press signed by thirty-nine women priests from Blackburn Diocese expressing their support for Philip's new appointment. Philip had cared for them, affirmed them, and keenly worked with them. It was, I believe, one of the saddest days in the Church of England over the last forty years when, because of intolerable pressure clearly hyped up by a few of the liberal establishment, this gifted young bishop with a heart for all people, especially the poor, withdrew his acceptance from what would have been an excellent appointment.

A few weeks after my evening meeting with women clergy, I was on the *'cathedra'* in the cathedral at the Eucharist to celebrate the tenth anniversary of the Ordination of the first women priests. The Dean of Women's Ministry presided at the Eucharist, and it was a joyful occasion. I recall having to take a few deep intakes of breath in the sermon preached by the Revd. Chris Nelson, who became one of our area deans. However, there was no apparent 'issue' over my not receiving Holy Communion - and, indeed, why should there ever be? No one except the celebrating priest is obliged to receive and, up until the mid-1960s, it was very common to have non-communicating Masses. As a young communicant, I was encouraged to receive Holy Communion at 8.00am on Sundays and to return at 11.00am for what was usually a non-communicating Solemn Eucharist.

The diocese was greatly blessed with two very fine Deans of Women's Ministry: Rachel Simper-Watts, who was in post when I arrived, and whom I later made an Honorary Canon; and Fleur Green, whom I also made an Honorary Canon. Both Fleur and Rachel were members of the bishop's staff and made a valuable contribution to our meetings and to the work of the staff team more generally.

My main disappointment was over the Chrism Eucharist; indeed, I had a fair measure of sympathy with those who felt that the way we managed this important diocesan event accentuated our differences. I inherited a situation where we had two Chrism Masses: one in the cathedral, with the diocesan bishop presiding, during which all priests were invited to renew their ordination vows; and a second, for those who in conscience could not renew their vows alongside women priest colleagues, presided over by the Bishop of Burnley, whom my predecessor had made Diocesan Episcopal Visitor. I was very pleased to honour that arrangement, but I said I would be attending that Mass, as well, and - seated on the 'Bishop's Chair' - preaching in alternate years. This arrangement was generally welcomed. I was Bishop to the whole Diocese, and I wanted to be with every deacon and priest as they renewed their vows. Endless hours were to be spent discussing how we did the Chrism Eucharist; in my second year, I appointed a commission to look at possible changes to the arrangements. I would have preferred for us all to gather in the cathedral, and for all male and female priests to renew their vows together.

I acknowledge that would be a compromise, but in the present dispensation some such compromises are called for on both sides. Above all else, I did not want some Anglo-Catholic clergy feeling they had to attend the Provincial Episcopal Visitor's (PEV) Chrism Mass because in conscience they were unable to renew their priestly ministry in company with both male and female clergy. While I fully support the appointment of, and the ministry of the PEVs (indeed, Catholic Anglicans would have been sunk without them), the diocese is the local Church and, within it, the diocesan bishop is the chief minister of word and sacrament, assisted in this ministry by his suffragan bishops; so I felt it would not serve the unity of the diocese if we could not all at least celebrate the Chrism Eucharist *in our own diocese with our bishop* and his suffragans. As much as I always looked forward to the Chrism Mass, I felt sad that we could not all stand together. Perhaps I was being too cautious, and, once again, trying too hard to come to a consensus. If I had insisted on having just one Chrism Eucharist, I wonder how many clergy would have 'defected' to the PEV Mass. However, the whole point was that we did not want to lose anyone from the local celebrations.

By the time of the installation and enthronement in the cathedral, I felt quite at home in the diocese, having visited a number of parishes, schools and key people in the area. I robed for that service in the mayor's parlour, and processed behind the clergy of the diocese through the main streets of the town to the Cathedral. When the west door was opened, the first person I noticed was a contemporary of mine from school. That seemed both an encouragement and a landmark, for it was at Elizabeth College that I first became aware of the inner stirring of a call to the ministerial priesthood - and here I was, now, the bishop of an extensive diocese, embarking on the biggest challenge of a journey that began when I was fifteen years old.

I processed alone down the length of the cathedral to the high altar, pausing seven times to remember my seven predecessors. At the altar, I exchanged the crozier presented to me by the Archdeaconry of Lewes and Hastings for the special silver bishop's crozier, carried only by the Bishop of Blackburn in his cathedral. It has been used in turn by each Bishop of Blackburn and was laid down, in anticipation of my arrival, by Bishop Alan, at his Farewell Thanksgiving Eucharist. This is a sign of continuity in the see - a point that I was always keen to emphasise. The incoming bishop does not 'turn on the tap', rather, he comes into a running stream. Certainly, he has the major role in determining where that stream will flow, but he is not a solo performer, and builds on what he has received from the past, as he works with his staff and clergy, and all those engaged in the prayer, life and work of the diocese.

In the course of the service, the bishop addresses the diocese; I stressed that our priority is to be a people open to God, and to let Him form us in holiness. I gave an illustration from the millennium fireworks at Lewes, where the crowd all shouted 'ooh' as the rockets went up and 'aaaah' as they exploded and came back down to earth. We needed to rediscover the oohs and aaahs in letting **God** search for us. The oohs pointed to the joys that lay ahead for us, and the aahs to those moments when we would find ourselves in a storm-tossed sea. I called for a new confidence in proclaiming the gospel in Lancashire, and for a shared sense of mission. I looked forward to being part of a diocese which lived out its life and faith in friendship with other faith communities. I assured members of other faith communities that, in concert with other Christian leaders, I would work to secure respect and honour for all people. I said that this would mean adopting a comprehensive agenda to tackle unjust social structures, prejudice (sometimes in subtle disguises), racism, poverty, bad housing, and environmental issues. I added that, together, we needed to respond firmly wherever we saw God's children being prevented from encountering His glory in His world. At the end of the service, I went outside to bless the town and county; and then to meet the congregation over lunch in King George's Hall.

As only a limited number of people from the Lancashire parishes could be accommodated at the installation service, there was an open invitation to attend a diocesan Eucharist at the cathedral four weeks later, on the eve of Pentecost. This was a more relaxed occasion, when we prayed especially for the guidance of God the Holy Spirit as we moved ahead in His power. Although I was already in post, with a full programme, these diocesan services did not complete

the launch of my episcopal ministry. I had arranged
to visit all fourteen deaneries for an evening Eucharist
and a question-and-answer session, followed by a social
event. The bishop's staff organised a comprehensive
induction programme, which enabled me to meet
key people in the diocese and region, including
opinion formers and the media. I also visited various
organisations and social projects. These included
government schemes such as partnership-funding,
community re-development, Sure Start and Family
Centres. The Board of Social Responsibility (as we
then called it) with its Director, Canon Chris Rich,
was conspicuously effective, and enabled us to provide
much-needed services in deprived parts of Lancashire.
I shall never forget going to a children's centre in East
Lancashire in their morning break, when they were
enjoying a warm snack; I enquired why the children
were having a fairly substantial meal close to lunchtime.
The answer was, that for some of those children this
represented their only hot meal of the day. Many of
them had no toys to play with at home - every penny
going to fuel their parents' drug habit.

I inherited a lively, talented and very hardworking staff,
and three of them - Bishop John Goddard of Burnley,
Dean Christopher Armstrong, and John Hawley, the
Archdeacon of Blackburn - were recent appointments.
They stayed with me throughout my time in Blackburn.
Bishop Stephen Pedley of Lancaster, who remained
for eighteen months, had been in charge during the
episcopal vacancy. It had been made clear to me
that the diocese was not looking for a bishop who

would 'rule by decree', but a bishop who would work collaboratively, and be a permission-giving leader. With a strong, gifted, and sparky team, I could see why that approach was right.

We tried various patterns for our meetings. For a while we even included in the staff team the Directors (as we then called them) of the Boards of Education, Ministry, Social Responsibility and Mission; but that made it a very large meeting. We always started with Matins and Mass, and the main meeting would usually finish with a two-course lunch, cooked by Christine. When she was catering for so many people every week, she felt one more meal a fortnight didn't make much difference.

I hope this does not sound sexist, but Christine and I have both said that we do not know how we would ever have coped if Christine had not given up her teaching when we moved. While Christine had many areas of interest, and gave support and care all around the diocese, we both felt very strongly that a ministry of welcome and hospitality at Bishop's House should be a particular mark of our pastoral ministry. Inevitably, rather too much fell on Christine's shoulders.

One afternoon, Christine invited someone to tea who had worked at Bishop's House in the 1970s; she revealed how many domestic staff there had been in those days. We had to run that big house, with its offices and chapel, supported only by Kathy Seed, who cleaned the whole place each week in half-a-day. We had the services of a gardener on two days a week; he initially served as my driver as well, but, as I was perfectly happy to drive myself on shorter trips, driving duties were later shared by Keith Thompson, the gardener, and Ray Noddle, who had been the Chief Constable's chauffeur. I enjoyed talking to them in the car, but discovered that I was able to work in the back seat - as also on the train.

As time went by, my visits to London increased; not infrequently it was necessary to stay, particularly when I attended the House of Lords for several days at a time. In the early days, with so much structural work taking place - particularly in the office and chapel area - we worked under siege conditions. Fr. Philip Gray, my chaplain, could not cope with the dust, and had to wear a face mask. The office staff took all the adversity that we encountered with good humour. I was blessed with my three chaplains: Philip, David Arnold, and Toby Webber who served in my last year.

I was equally blessed with other personal staff: my principal secretary, Sue Taylor, a half-time assistant secretary, Hilary Wilby, and Margaret Ashton, the part-time bursar. Not only were they efficient, loyal and supportive, but they understood my ways of working, and my shortcomings. They were fun to work with and seemed to enjoy it when I wound them up – at least, most of the time; Sue only got angry with me once. It was the first day of April, and the offices and filing room were not as tidy as they might have been. I announced that the Church Commissioners had rung early to say that the new First Church Estates Commissioner was travelling with his team from York to Carlisle and that they would stop off at Bishop's House to inspect our relatively new office set-up. Everyone set to, and at 11.45 Sue said, 'They're a bit late.' When I responded that the whole exercise was an April Fool, she really was livid and Hilary told me to 'get out'. I laughed all the way back to my office.

Bishop's House was, with few exceptions, a very happy working environment; the occasional social events with my personal staff and their spouses were always accompanied by much laughter. Joining us on those occasions, and in the office from time-to-time, was my assistant chaplain, Becky Hollis, who was succeeded by Julie Jones and then by Nancy Goodrich, each serving in their curacy. They assisted on liturgical occasions, and at other events; Julie provided wider support assisting with Mission Action Planning reports, for instance. I was pleased that she subsequently combined her first incumbency with the role of Deanery Missioner. For her part, Nancy helped me to research my House of Lords speeches, providing support in that area of my activity; she became a parish priest in the north of the Diocese just before I retired.

The long-overdue and much-needed improvements to the fabric of Bishop's House caused inconvenience in the early days, but it proved to be well worth it. I was delighted with the clear glass in the chapel, replacing frosted glass window panes – making the chapel light and airy; it enabled us to look out over the beautiful

Lancashire countryside, praising God for His world, which He created through His Son and redeemed by Him. Our new nave altar was simple but dignified; the Confraternity of the Blessed Sacrament gave us a hanging pyx in which to reserve the Blessed Sacrament; and a Statue of Our Lady of Walsingham was donated by a local Walsingham cell.

The chapel was central to our life, and, I believe, to the life of the diocese. The chaplain and I would recite Matins and Evensong daily, and we celebrated a daily Mass, seldom with fewer than four from the house and office in attendance. Frequently I was celebrating the Eucharist elsewhere in the diocese; the house Mass was then celebrated by the chaplain. Occasionally, I would license clergy in the chapel, welcome groups from the diocese to join me in worship, and hold a variety of other services there.

Some two months after I arrived, I attended my first three-day meeting of the House of Bishops, in Liverpool: forty-four diocesan bishops and nine elected suffragan bishops. Among the items on the agenda was the consecration of women (which was to come up at most subsequent meetings); the Archbishop of York (David Hope) spoke on Mission Action Planning (MAP) - how it had been implemented when he was Bishop of London, and how it was being received in the Diocese of York. It seemed to me that this was exactly what we needed in Blackburn. I spoke to him after the session, and he agreed to send me further material. A couple of weeks later, I went with John

Hawley, the Archdeacon of Blackburn, to a meeting of the Diocesan Action Zone Group (DAZ) at St. Anne's Woodplumpton, where Damian Feeney - a very keen, mission-focused priest - had just been instituted. Also present were Simon Bessant, the Diocesan Missioner, and Mike Chew, a lay representative from St. John's Baxenden, formerly quality director of the electrical conglomerate, Philips. Mike had taken early retirement, and longed to see the Church renewed; he had a passion for mission and evangelism.

2007. Mission visit to a school during one of the Mission weeks.

I told the DAZ Group about the Archbishop's talk at the House of Bishops meeting. They, too, were very positive about the promotion of Mission Action Planning. In fact, everything about that afternoon was hopeful and encouraging - there was so much enthusiasm around. It was as if God the Holy Spirit had fallen afresh on us. MAP in Blackburn Diocese was clearly 'born' that afternoon. A little later, I had my first meeting of the Diocesan Synod; in speaking about mission, I said that it must be at the heart of our life together as a diocese and that every parish needed to draw up a MAP. This is how I ended my address: 'However weak, however humble we may be, whether we have lots of gifts or few, or even wonder if we have any at all, we are all called to share in the saving work of Christ's Mission to His world. I rejoice to be sharing this work with you, and I ask that through our love, our prayer and involvement each one of us will carry our share of the responsibility laid on the Church in this Diocese to announce the Kingdom and make disciples.'

Exactly six months after my episcopal ordination, a residential clergy conference was organised at the College of St. Hild and St. Bede in Durham. This afforded a valuable opportunity for me to be with the clergy, to pray with them, to learn and discuss with them, to sit down and talk with them, and to socialise with them. I restricted my major contribution to a sermon at the concluding Eucharist in the cathedral, and an address on the second day.

By the time of the conference, I had completed my official induction programme, paid a visit to eighty parishes, and completed two-thirds of my deanery visits. Blackburn Diocese comprises practically the whole of Lancashire, referring to itself as 'The Church of England in Lancashire' – I had some satisfaction, therefore, that I had visited every part of the diocese at least once. At the final conference dinner, I was touched to be presented with a cut-glass, engraved tankard to mark my first clergy conference. The evaluation sheets indicated that it had been a successful conference and I received a number of warm and appreciative letters. In truth, it was the conference that marked the real end of my induction process.

To return to the substance of what was discussed in Durham: my session with the clergy had the title, 'The Bishop – the first six months'. As tempting as it was to turn the session into a 'justification by works' - having just come through one of the most demanding, busy, and scary times in my whole ministry - I resisted, and looked to the future. I chose to focus on two sentences from the Archbishop's Charge, delivered to me the night before my Consecration, that also appeared in the Statement of Needs submitted by the Diocese to the Crown Appointments' Commission: 'The Bishop would see that the decline in church attendance is unacceptable, and that as a top priority he will seek to reverse these trends and lead the diocese into growth.' Doing nothing was clearly not an option, and there had to be some re-setting of the compass. Following my installation sermon, I focused on the importance of waiting on God and the need for renewal in our devotional discipline. I argued that the creative thinking that had taken place in the previous 'Vision' document and elsewhere in the diocese, should be aligned with the emerging diocesan strategy; each parish should then work up its own Mission Action Plans. My aim was to encourage as much local initiative as possible, without the heavy hand of the bishop controlling everything - but I did want to be visible as a helping hand.

I urged the clergy to remember that the mission is never truly ours - but always, first and foremost, God's - and I reminded them of the statement recently quoted to us by Simon Bessant, our Director of Mission and Evangelism, that it is not that the Church of God has a Mission, but that the God of Mission has a Church, and for that reason, prayer and worship are always essential to all that we do in His name. That was to be the hallmark of all our endeavour over the next eight-and-a-half years. Looking on now, from a distance, I am grateful that this imperative is still followed in the diocese, albeit with some inevitable changes of emphasis.

10 THE SEE: SOMETIMES STORM TOSSED
Blackburn (2)

Any former Diocesan Bishop could write a thick volume on his time in his see. While my life may not have been important, I do not intend to follow Bishop Hensley Henson of Durham (1863-1947) who, in *Retrospect of an Unimportant Life*, required three volumes to write his autobiography. In this short memoir, many of the exciting and important happenings from the Blackburn years regrettably have to be consigned to the margins. However, we do not forget that the margins are where the wild flowers grow, and memories of those events, and the people who were part of them, are fertile and exciting to revisit personally. For all bishops the care of the clergy must come first.

We were a large diocese, but the suffragan bishops did not have an area delegated to them by legislation. We had an understanding that the suffragans would be more immediately responsible for the day-to-day running of the two archdeaconries with the two archdeacons, and that I worked across the whole diocese. All the clergy had direct access to me, and I made it clear that I was not simply to be regarded as 'the last port of call'. I tried to be as accessible as possible, and, even if I couldn't solve problems, at least I could listen to them. Surely the bishop's calling is to be a listener who is with the people.

The suffragans and archdeacons also had a wealth of

experience, mostly in parochial ministry, and therefore understood the difficulties and pressures to which the clergy were subject. These were particularly difficult times for the clergy. I acknowledge that to complain about the culture is rather like a sailor complaining about the rough sea; but the fact remains that we minister in a very exacting climate. We have seen the change coming for decades, but the general perception of the Church, and attitude to the Christian Faith, is a long way from where it was when I started in the Black Country in 1973. There are many challenging areas in the Blackburn Diocese, and they are by no means all in urban areas. In addition, there is the task of raising funds – in particular to meet the Parish Share (the Common Fund to pay, house, and train all the clergy, and to pay the central costs of running the diocese).

Visit of Archbishop of Canterbury to the Diocese. Dean of Blackburn, Christopher Armstrong, Archbishop, N.R., Jack Straw, Foreign Secretary and MP for Blackburn.

While I was in Blackburn, there seemed to be a stream of new legislation coming from the General Synod – including the Clergy Terms of Service and the Clergy Discipline Measure - which left many clergy feeling somewhat beleaguered. Although positive in itself, the Clergy Terms of Service Measure meant that all under Common Tenure (and those already in post who elected to retain the freehold, were encouraged to join in) would be required to undergo a review of ministry. I was given much assistance over several years by Sandra Cobbin, who had been brought in to help us manage change, and who would work with Canon Andrew Clitherow, a very gifted Director of Training. Quite swiftly, we were able to develop a review scheme which combined peer group and senior staff appraisal and drew favourable comment when Sandra and I presented it to a symposium at King's College, London.

Bishop's Staff residential 'The Team' 2008.

While accepting the real limitations of the 1963 Ecclesiastical Jurisdiction Measure, and the need for something new, I cannot speak with great enthusiasm about the Clergy Discipline Measure (CDM). This consumed an enormous amount of my time, particularly when it was first introduced, as there were a number of new matters – significantly, including historic issues – which were now dealt with through this legislation. Accepting the cards you are dealt is part of being a bishop, and there is a constant need to be prepared for challenges coming from every direction. What I was not prepared for were complaints under the CDM being made against me. In fact, three of us on the staff had formal complaints made against us. At one time, I had three against me running concurrently, including one from Chichester Diocese going back over fifteen years to the time when I was still a rural dean. All of these, including those against my colleagues, were adjudicated by the Archbishop of York, and were all dismissed, but we had to have legal representation, and it all cost the Church of England money.

For the most part, I possess the kind of make-up that enables me just to get on with life when difficulties occur, and I am thankful for this. Bishops encounter so many troubling situations that I generally took the view that when the dustbin is full, a bit more on top does not make much difference. Christopher Armstrong, the dean, said the deeper the difficulty the broader my smile. All that may be true, but it is no use pretending that the personal cost is nil, and that it does not affect one's wife and family. Many clergy were not able just to 'carry on as normal', knowing that there was a formal complaint against them; particularly when the allegation was of a serious nature, and the 'neutral act' of standing down from all duties is required. There were two aspects of the legislation that I regarded as totally unacceptable for the clergy: the length of time the process took, and the way that the legislation was used as a vehicle for the disaffected and those hoping to be rid of their parish priest.

Another worry I had about the CDM concerned the role of the bishop. He is both the chief pastor, and, as the ordination service for a bishop reminds us, 'with the Shepherd's love he is to be merciful, but with firmness: to minister discipline, but with compassion'. The CDM required the bishop, when he had received the report from the appropriate legal officer, to decide on the penalty, if there were to be one. In turn, that meant that the bishop had to withdraw from any pastoral involvement with the priest concerned during the whole process under adjudication. I regard this as most unsatisfactory, and have experience of just how difficult rebuilding a relationship with a priest can be when it looks as though his or her bishop deserted them at the very time they most needed support from their chief pastor. Lessons have been learned, however, and I dare to hope that this aspect of the Clergy Discipline Measure now works more satisfactorily, though concerns are still being voiced.

I am often asked what I enjoyed most about being the chief pastor: 'to be with the people of God and with the clergy in the parishes and churches of the diocese and presiding at the Eucharist' is always my answer. One of my chaplains said that he always knew when I had a confirmation in the evening, as there was a spring in my step during the afternoon. I am grateful that - even now, in retirement - I am still asked by bishops to undertake occasional confirmations, and so to exercise this special ministry. For confirmation is a great mission event: a celebration of the Holy Spirit in completion of the Church's rite of initiation; and a unique opportunity to preach and to talk to those who have joined us for this great occasion, and who have had little previous contact with the Church.

In line with my three priorities from the enthronement sermon - Prayer, Holiness and Mission – our diocesan Mission Action Plan initiative [MAP] was formally launched in the cathedral on the first anniversary of my episcopal ordination. In asking parishes to draw up their own MAP, I wanted to lead by example by producing my own MAP, in order to communicate what would be my priorities for myself, for the bishop's staff, and for the diocesan staff and departments. Within a year, eighty-five percent of parishes had submitted their MAPs. A second bishop's MAP was published the following year, and I sent out one of my regular mailings to the clergy to ask them to repeat their mission planning process.

We took a major step by encouraging the clergy to take their vision for growth 'into their bloodstream', and inviting them to attend the national four-day course 'Leading your Church into Growth'. This significant venture was supported by a Mission Action Plan Working Group in which Mike Chew (the facilitator and director) was joined by the Director of Mission and Evangelism and Director of Continuing Ministerial Education (Simon Bessant); the Director of Ministry and Training (Canon Andrew Clitherow) who worked tirelessly to encourage and renew the ministry of the clergy; and Fr. Damian Feeney (Vicar of Woodplumpton and, later, Assistant Diocesan Missioner). This group merits high praise for the guidance and impetus it lent to the project, extending its reach to places that we never expected to bring within our ambit. I was delighted that Mike Chew became a lay canon in 2008.

Once the MAP had been embedded in the life of the diocese, it was a natural step for its work to be integrated into the appropriate diocesan structures: the Discipleship and Ministry Department, the Parish Mission Support Department, and the Board of Education. At the same time the Bishop's Mission Action Plan was developed further by another initiative, 'Going for Growth', and a linked Vision Statement, 'Growing in Faith and Prayer: Transforming Communities in The Power of The Holy Spirit'. The suffragan bishops, the archdeacons, and I worked our way round the whole diocese spending time in each parish, leading mission activity. The aim of these days was to 'grow in' to God and 'grow out' in love and service and sharing the Good News of Jesus Christ; accordingly, we called them 'Growing up, Growing out Days'.

I wish I could write at greater length about MAPs. I would refer readers to the book written by Mike Chew and Archdeacon Mark Ireland (now Archdeacon of Blackburn) *Mission Action Planning* (SPCK, 2009), with ten pages devoted exclusively to the Blackburn journey. The book also provides evidence of the growth that came about in parishes that took MAP seriously. It also described the enhanced improvement that could be seen when the MAP project was led by a priest who had attended the 'Leading Your Church into Growth' course. Canon Mike Chew concludes his chapter on the Blackburn MAP like this: 'The overall conclusion for the Blackburn Diocese is that the Growth Strategy/MAP initiative has made a significant difference to the attendance trend for usual Sunday attendance, especially for those churches that responded positively to the Bishop's call for Mission Action Plans.' I would want to add that these figures did not include the increasing number of weekday services - especially Messy Church - and the discernible change in the 'culture' of the diocese.

In all honesty, the bishop's staff was initially rather lukewarm about MAPs. Some in the diocese considered this to be a strange road for a bishop with a Catholic background to choose. From the outset, the most enthusiastic member of staff was Archdeacon John Hawley, who became part of the initial MAP group. As we moved towards the launch, and as I invited Mike Chew into more staff meetings, the team started to seek more active involvement in the planning - from that point, I felt that we had all embraced the vision, and, as with all the other projects, we pulled together.

We lost two strong members of the staff team in the first eighteen months of my episcopate. Colin Williams had been a hardworking, wise, clear-thinking and efficient Archdeacon of Lancaster; he was a keen ecumenicist and was appointed as General Secretary of the Conference of European Churches in Geneva. Bishop Stephen, a much-loved Bishop of Lancaster, retired; he was what can only be described as a 'mega-pastor'- wise but with a gift for seeing the funny side of things. Our Diocesan Secretary, Canon Michael Wedgeworth, always supportive, left a little later; he had steered the diocese through changing times, not least a major refurbishment of Whalley Abbey, our retreat and conference centre. He was replaced by Graeme Pollard, who was no stranger to the diocese, although at the time working in the Diocese of Truro. This was an excellent appointment, a strong member of the staff team, very hard working, highly respected and in tune with our vision for the diocese, and another one with a keen sense of humour. Bishop Stephen was replaced by Canon Geoff Pearson, Vicar of a large and thriving Evangelical parish in Liverpool and Area Dean of Huyton; he was a great colleague, a fine pastor and missioner and a real encourager. With characteristic generosity he agreed to 'multi task' and, with his wife Jean, a reader and lay minister, to work the local parish. Geoff thus also became Priest in Charge of St. James's, Shireshead.

Colin was replaced as Archdeacon by Canon Peter Ballard, our Director of Education. Peter asked if he could also continue as Director of Education, by sharing certain responsibilities among the education team, and agreeing a job share with John, his fellow Archdeacon. He presented his idea to me as a way of setting an example throughout the diocese: cutting senior posts at a time when parishes, too, were being asked to save posts. The workload of the Director of Education, alone, was exceedingly heavy: Blackburn had more church schools than any diocese outside London, with one-hundred-and-eighty primary schools and ten secondary schools. Peter had assembled a strong and dedicated team in the Board of Education, but it was still not wise for the director's post to be part-time. I should probably not have agreed to it, although Peter managed the responsibilities of both posts, and was always readily available to address any problem in the diocese. My regular visits to the schools gave ample evidence of the fruits of Peter's work with the Board of Education. Those visits were among my happiest experiences in the diocese, and time spent with the staff and pupils manifested my interest, support and encouragement. My involvement with the schools left me wishing that I had given more time to this work when I was a parish priest.

Much happened at the cathedral during my occupancy of the see. We were privileged to have four royal visits, including one from Her Majesty the Queen, on a civic visit to Blackburn, when I was able to present the dean and some of the cathedral canons to the Queen. We had a special service for the Queen's Diamond Jubilee, and Festival Eucharists for the visits to the diocese of the Archbishop of Canterbury and of the Archbishop of York. The Member of Parliament for Blackburn, Jack Straw, brought the American Secretary of State, Condoleezza Rice, to the cathedral when he was Foreign Secretary.

Each year, there were important services in the cathedral, including the ordination of deacons and confirmations. The standard of music was always very high, with numerous choral events; it is worthy of note that the junior choir included children from disadvantaged backgrounds, who received general support.

I conducted a full visitation to the cathedral over ten days, and was assisted by a small team led by the Rt. Revd. Geoffrey Turner, formerly Bishop of Stockport.

One significant feature of the work of the cathedral in my time, was the creation of the Exchange Development Agency, to promote community cohesion, education and outreach. It was led by Canon Chris Chivers, now Principal of Westcott House, Cambridge, assisted by Anjum Anwar, a Muslim teacher who had been appointed as Dialogue Development Officer at the cathedral in 2007. Both Anjum and Chris had a wider role in the promotion of interfaith dialogue at home and abroad. They were among those who supported and advised me when I took my place in the House of Lords, enabling me to have a voice on social justice issues for the County of Lancashire.

The Temple Lectures, delivered in the Cathedral, on contemporary social and ethical issues, were inaugurated in my time by Canon Chris Chivers, Canon Chancellor - to honour Archbishop William Temple of Canterbury, who had created the Blackburn Diocese in 1926, when he was Bishop of Manchester. I found these of great interest, and enjoyed meeting and providing hospitality to the distinguished lecturers.

It is well known in cathedral circles that relations between the bishop and the dean are not always of the best. Since the time of the Reformation, the diocese and the cathedral have been economically and structurally distinct. The bishop comes in to ordain and to confirm; the statutes usually provide for him to preach three or four times a year - and, if he wishes, to carry out a visitation - and at other times, by request or invitation. Interestingly, people talk to the bishop about 'your cathedral'. I used to point out that the only part that is mine is the cathedra, the bishop's throne; even though the cathedral may be 'the hut of the shepherd', the Bishop has no legal right to come and go there as he pleases - although in my happy experience, I was always given a warm reception.

While it is true that there are tensions in Anglicanism, we are good at living with it; in my case, relations between the bishop and cathedral were generally good. The dean, Christopher Armstrong, and I had much in common, having both trained at a monastic college, and were ordained around the same time; and we also had some 'good disagreement'. Chris was well read, reflective, and always had the ability to see an issue or a suggestion from other angles, and he was very generous. We met together every six weeks for breakfast and to pray the Daily Office, and to talk about the cathedral and the diocese. Chris was a good critical friend and a source of encouragement; he and his wife, Geraldine, were kind and most hospitable. Although a week seldom passed when I did not have reason to travel the four miles to the cathedral, I regret, in some ways, that I did not devote more time to the cathedral and its community – although I would never wish this to have been at the expense of time spent with the clergy and people in the parishes.

Christine and I made the first of many visits to Braunschweig, our linked Lutheran diocese in Lower Saxony, in mid-2005. We already had six parish partnerships with them, as well as social responsibility links, youth links, teacher partnerships, and close links between our cathedrals, clergy, readers and lay ministers. We also had regular rounds of theological discussion, and were delighted when Pastor Woldermar Flake and his wife, Pastor Sabine, and their two young children, Henry and Elsa, came for nearly three years to live and minister in the parish of Trawden, and its associated parishes in the Colne and Villages Team Ministry. Bishop Friedrich Weber and his wife, Bielda, were among our German partners who became very good friends. We were greatly saddened when Bishop Friedrich died, in 2015, shortly after retiring. On our visits to Saxony we always visited the Christian Youth Village Movement (CJD) at Salzgitter, for those with learning difficulties, and employed in making small parts for Volkswagen. It was a joy to welcome a group from CJD to Lancashire, when they stayed at our retreat centre at Whalley Abbey.

Christine with children from Sunflower House, Bloemfontein.

Our other Link Diocese - the Diocese of the Free State in South Africa (formerly called the Diocese of Bloemfontein) - happened to be the longest-lasting such link in the Anglican Communion. We made two visits there with groups from the diocese. The first of these was led by Fr. Simon Aitken, Vicar of Longridge (who later went out to be Sub-Dean of Bloemfontein Cathedral and then Dean of Kimberley); the other visit included a large group of young people, and was enormous fun. The Bishop of the Free State, Paddy Glover, and his wife Kirsty, became good friends of ours, as did the dean, Don Narraway, and his wife Pat. We can never forget the joy of the South African people in worship, or their generous hospitality – in the townships, a wonderful meal would be prepared for us by those who were going short themselves. Perhaps the most moving experience was entering a hospice for the dying with our young people when we visited a ward and prayed with the patients. By the time we reached the end of the ten-bed ward, the first patient had died. When we left the ward, we were told that the hospice was closing in a fortnight for lack of funds.

The Mosamaria Aids Ministry and the Sunflower House for children with life-limiting conditions were keenly supported by the Diocese of Blackburn and were close to our hearts - Joan Marston, the founder of Sunflower House, being made one of our lay canons. Although distance and cost prevented frequent exchanges, occasional, much-valued reciprocal visits were made.

This was the first time that Christine and I had visited South Africa, and the country and especially the Diocese of the Free State retain a big place in our hearts and prayers. I am pleased that Bishop Paddy's successor has one of my mitres to wear. I often wear a pectoral cross given to me by the Free State when I was consecrated.

We treated these visits to the Free State as pilgrimages,

and they were grace-filled times, which had a deep effect on us all. Christians are a pilgrim people who journey to the Father through this life with Jesus Christ in the power of the Holy Spirit; we look forward to seeing Him face-to-face after death. From early times Christians have travelled to holy places as a means of growing in holiness, to aid us on our journey to the heavenly kingdom. We travel in company with the Lord, who made his own pilgrimage to Jerusalem to suffer and die for us. Many parishes in Blackburn went on pilgrimage, particularly to the Shrine of Our Lady of Walsingham, which I have visited every year since my ordination.

Before lunch with the Ecumenical Patriarch in Istanbul 2006.
L to R. N.R., Bishop John Hind of Chichester, - Senior Chaplain to
the Ecumenical Patriarch

In company with fellow pilgrims from the diocese, I led two pilgrimages to Turkey, the first of which was with Bishop John Hind and Chichester Diocese. I shall never forget the Anglican Pilgrimage to Lourdes with the Society of Mary, led by Archbishop Rowan Williams and eight Anglican Bishops, accompanied by Cardinal Kasper, in his position as President of the Pontifical Council for Promoting Christian Unity. One of the most impressive features of this visit was the absolute priority given to the sick - my abiding memory is that no matter who you are, or whatever you are doing, nothing can be allowed to get in the way of loving and caring for the sick.

150th anniversary of Our Lady's appearance at Lourdes. N.R. back row on the right. Front row, third from left Archbishop of Canterbury. On his left Cardinal Kasper, from the Pontifical Council for Promoting Christian Unity.

There was a keen ecumenical spirit shared by the denominations in Lancashire with relations between them co-ordinated by Churches Together in Lancashire (CTL); and for much of my time among them, that group funded two posts, a CTL secretary, and an Interfaith Relations Officer, a post reflecting the diversity of the area. Church leaders gave a high priority to our meetings, and in our early days we had an annual residential meeting. We sought to make our ecumenical endeavours project-based, so that we could work together, rather than merely coming together to talk. This contributed to the warmth, generosity, and sense of mutual commitment that were established between us.

Strangely, Blackburn Cathedral had no ecumenical canons. In 2008, I rectified this by appointing the Revd. Stephen Poxon, Chair of the North Lancashire Methodist District, and subsequently, President of the Methodist Conference, as the first ecumenical canon of the cathedral. He was joined by Dr Friedrich Weber (Bishop of Braunschweig), and Canon Kevin Kenny (Roman Catholic Dean of Blackburn with Darwen, and Canon of the Holy Sepulchre Jerusalem - one of the least denominationally-minded people I know). I particularly appreciated Kevin's kind and helpful telephone calls on a couple of occasions when I ran into trouble with the media.

I rejoiced that the diocese accepted and worked for all its people, irrespective of their spiritual needs and physical location. The support for rural communities, for which my predecessor had worked so hard, was sustained – many of these continued to suffer the consequences of the foot and mouth epidemic. Rural poverty in Lancashire was certainly a serious issue. One of our centres of Higher and Further Education was Myerscough College (formerly Lancashire College of Agriculture) which provided land-based and sports courses for some eight thousand students, and with which I had some involvement. The college supported an Anglican chaplaincy. Such experience meant that I was able to ask questions and to speak on some rural matters affecting Lancashire, in the House of Lords. And it is significant that the first Honorary Canon of the Cathedral whom I appointed was the Revd. Roger Hamblin, who had served for over thirty years in rural parishes, including eight years as an agricultural chaplain.

The dedicated rural clergy, many of whom stayed in the county for most of their ministry, were vitally important to the work of the diocese; the majority of rural parishes were in the Lancaster Archdeaconry, and this rural parochial ministry was strongly supported both by the Bishops of Lancaster (Stephen Pedley and Geoff Pearson) and by the Archdeacons (Colin Williams, Peter Ballard and Michael Everitt). I also had a strong team, not only among the staff, but also among the area deans. Much of the work in the Archdeaconry of Blackburn, based in the area south of the River Ribble, was of a different nature, but undertaken by an equally dedicated clergy. The Archdeacon of Blackburn, John Hawley, was an experienced urban parish priest with an insatiable appetite for work – he appeared only to take time off for one round of golf each week. Bishop John Goddard was a gifted and energetic Bishop of Burnley, always on top of his brief and with an excellent knowledge of the clergy and parishes in the south of the diocese. For much of my time, he was an elected suffragan bishop on the General Synod of the Church of England and came with me to the House of

Bishops. Vivienne Goddard, Bishop John's wife, also sat on the General Synod, and has worked faithfully and very hard for the diocese since their arrival in 1992. She has served for a long time on General Synod, and is a keen member of the Catholic Group, speaking firmly and courageously - and not just on the contentious ecclesiological issues the church has faced in the last two decades.

Bishop John was much respected by Muslim communities and by those of other faiths. In the northern province, in the north-west region, and nationally, he was widely consulted on interfaith and social-urban issues. He always spoke out fearlessly against the evil of racism, and all forms of injustice. Within the diocese as a whole, there was a wider team working on interfaith issues; we received a warm welcome in many of the mosques, in the offices of the Lancashire Council of Mosques, and in the College of Islamic Knowledge and Guidance *(Jamiatul Ilm Wal Huda)*, where I was invited to present the awards on one occasion, and where I visited from time to time. The Hindu temple in Preston also welcomed us, and I was invited to address the synagogue in Blackpool. The Anglican and Muslim Group (set up by my predecessor and Lord Patel) met three times a year, either at Bishop's House or at the Lancashire Council of Mosques. An agenda was agreed beforehand, and matters of mutual concern and interest were discussed.

The diocese worked in partnership with statutory and voluntary bodies for community cohesion and the relief of poverty. Of the fourteen local authorities in Blackburn Diocese, seven were in the most deprived thirty percent in the country and Blackburn with Darwen, Blackpool, and Burnley were in the ten percent most deprived. In order to respond more effectively, the diocese brought together its work on mission and social action within a new Parish Mission Support Department. The Revd. Dave Banbury, an experienced evangelist, was appointed as the departmental leader and Diocesan Missioner; he was thoughtful, dynamic, energetic – and had a delightful wit. A linked appointment was that of the Revd. Ed Saville to be Lead Officer for Social Responsibility - underlining that Social Action and Mission belonged together, and that Mission and Social Justice are both works for - and of - the Kingdom. Ed Saville's vision and mine were very similar; I also remain grateful for his help and assistance in briefing me for media interviews and drafting speeches for the House of Lords. If I made any sort of mark in the public arena on social issues, it was certainly with his help (and that of Martyn Halsall, the Communications Officer). In truth this is part of the wider sense of gratitude I feel for the work undertaken by the Board of Social Responsibility and by its successor body, the Parish Mission Support department.

There was frequent criticism for those of us who spoke out about poverty and deprivation - but what else was to be expected of us, as Church leaders? We were in an area of continuous economic decline – a quarter of the children within the diocese were living below the poverty line, and Blackpool had notably high mortality rates for young men and for adult males overall. One Good Friday evening, I remember being surprised to see my face in the regional news headlines with that of the Chancellor of the Exchequer, George Osborne: in criticising the coalition government cutbacks, I had called upon ministers to stand by those who were socially and economically at risk – adding that we needed to search seriously for a new way of valuing individuals. Once again the cry went up that 'the bishops should keep out of politics'. My consistent response was that God's Kingdom embraces not just the Church, but the whole world. The Church, and indeed all Faith communities, has a right, and a duty, to make a proper contribution to the life of our democracy. My colleagues and I urged the people of Lancashire to reject the politics of hate, and to shun political parties and pressure groups that preached division and hatred. Before the 2010 General Election I argued that 'Hate will not repay one penny of the money the banks lost in 2008. Hate isn't going to build one single affordable home. Hate isn't going to solve a single crime. Hate isn't going to help a single university student with a big loan he or she needs just to get through the course. Hate isn't going to reopen a closed Accident and Emergency Unit.'

Just before I retired, I was asked 'What have been the major stresses and strains of being the Bishop?' I replied, 'Dealing with serious problems, and there have been quite a few. I have a notice on my board in my office saying that "being a bishop is like white-water rafting; you're always worried what set of boulders will come up next" – and it's true. I also have to say the pace of change has not been easy to manage, but I have good colleagues to help with that.'

But at the end of the day, being Bishop of the Diocese means that the buck stops with you. It is also a stress to have to travel to London and other places very regularly. Again, it is the divided loyalties. A bishop is not just bishop of the diocese but in that capacity, he also has central and national responsibilities that take him away from the diocese.

11   IN AND OUT OF THE SEE - Blackburn(3)

Bishops must spend much time out of their dioceses, not because they want to escape from them, but because it is part of their job. The bishop is 'wedded' to the diocese, but he is also a bishop in the Church of God, and a member of the college of bishops, sharing in the governance of and service to the wider Church. This, in part, involves regular meetings with fellow bishops and assuming some central responsibilities. Our Church is 'by law established', obliging bishops to seek to forge robust links with society in general. It is essential, therefore, that the bishop has a strong team in the diocese; I was fortunate in this respect. The excellent diocesan team in Blackburn was headed by two suffragan bishops – each with wider responsibilities of their own. The House of Bishops – comprising all forty-four diocesan bishops with nine suffragan bishops elected by their peers – normally met for its residential meeting three or four times a year. The suffragans as a group met with all the diocesan bishops on an annual basis, which is a meeting of the College of Bishops – that is, all diocesan and suffragan bishops in the Church of England.

Much of the work of the House was routine – inevitably, some of it not very interesting. The meetings always had their high spots: Archbishop Rowan Williams was consistently rewarding to listen to, and his devotional addresses were always of exceptional quality. If any bishops wished to contribute to the discussions in the main sessions, this was usually possible. I was initially unsure about addressing such an august gathering, but I soon 'found my feet'. These were particularly challenging times, on several fronts, and I believe that we listened to each another with respect. Traditional Catholics in the House formed but a small minority, but our grouping included some good speakers, and two of the finest theological minds in the House.

I was not viewed as a narrow or 'single-issue' man; while I did speak on ecclesiological issues, I also tended to speak on urban issues, deprivation and poverty - issues that concerned Lancashire. I enjoyed the company of my fellow bishops and the informal discussions in the margins of the main sessions.

It was especially good to reflect and pray with brother bishops at these gatherings. We all met for the Daily Offices and the Eucharist, each day. At the annual meeting at Hinsley Hall in Leeds, some ten bishops would pray silently in the Blessed Sacrament Chapel for a while before Matins. When I became concerned about the direction of travel of the Church of England, I often thought back to those especially rich times in that deeply prayerful corner, early in the morning. Retiring bishops are usually invited by the archbishops to preach at the Eucharist at their final House of Bishops meeting. I introduced into that address two of my 'heroes', Bishop Edward King (ob. 1910) and Archbishop Michael Ramsey (ob. 1988). During that meeting, further discussion had taken place on the ordination of women to the episcopate and provision for those who in conscience could not accept this departure from the great tradition of the undivided Church of the East and the West. Towards the end of my address, and aided by Michael Ramsey, I summarised one aspect of my abiding understanding of the nature of the Church of England: 'I make no comment on what we have decided this week except to say that I believe we do show the Lord to His world when we are being true, not to compromise, but to the comprehensive nature of the Anglican Church as we live the life of Christ's body. Seventy-five years ago, Michael Ramsey wrote in *The Gospel and the Catholic Church*: "For while the Anglican Church is vindicated by its place in history, the strikingly balanced witness to Gospel and Church and sound learning, its greater vindication lies in its pointing through its own history to something of which it is a fragment. Its credentials are its incompleteness, with the tension and the travail in its soul. It is clumsy and untidy, it baffles neatness and logic. For it is sent, not to commend itself as the best type of Christianity, but by its brokenness to point to the universal church wherein all have died." Despite all of its problems, the Church of England, with its glory and brokenness and with its full catholicity and full evangelicalism, continues to witness to one Church. Surely, when this face of the Church is seen, we reflect the body of Christ.'

I was pleased to take leave of the House with those words. I had made warm friendships across the wide spectrum of the church and found support - especially from the small group of Catholic bishops and from my cell group. Bishops were encouraged to join support groups with other bishops, usually those consecrated around the same time. I was the only traditionalist in my cell group, but, with one exception, we all came from a Catholic background. There was a real commitment to each other, and I think we all became friends. It was a meeting I would not miss. We all became bishops at about the same time, met in each other's dioceses, made our own agenda - which always included prayer, Eucharist, lectio divina (meditative reading of sacred scripture), an afternoon outing, plenty of group discussion, and a good dinner. It was a time for sharing our joys and sorrows openly and learning from each other – with our guard down.

All members of the House of Bishops are *ex-officio* members of the General Synod, which meets two or three times each year. As mentioned earlier, in 1995, I had been elected by the Chichester diocesan clergy to the General Synod, so I was familiar with its workings. Although I entered fully into the life of the Synod, I have to say that it was without much enthusiasm. I certainly enjoyed the company of the members of all three Houses of the Synod, but I did not miss the actual meetings and ploughing through the mass of preparatory paperwork when I retired.

At my final Synod, in an undeservedly-generous assessment of my time as Bishop of Blackburn, the Archbishop of York advanced his view that I had the most distinctive voice in the whole of the General Synod. I spoke at most sessions, and always had a few speeches prepared - but a bishop standing to speak is

not automatically called, unlike in other parts of the
Anglican Communion.

Although I made some of my better speeches on
social issues, I am aware that it is the stance that I
adopted during my time as Bishop of Blackburn
on the ordination of women to the priesthood and
episcopate that is of interest. It is a position that I
have always held, and continue to hold. In an early
speech to the General Synod, as a bishop, I included
the following: 'I still cannot see where a Bishop of the
Universal Church – and that is what Bishops of the
Church of England are – finds his authority from to
take part in the consecration of a woman. I understand
the consecration of women to be inconsistent with
the historic tradition of the Church, and it is clear it
would be detrimental to our ecumenical relations
with, in particular, the Orthodox and Roman Catholic
Churches. And yet – and I do not intend in any way
to be patronising – I have worked joyfully with women
priests in two dioceses, and if we somehow turned the
clock back to pre-1993, I know the Diocese I now
serve, and the whole Church of England would be
hugely impoverished. ... But then, I know if we were
to move forward now (to consecrate women) we would
actually lose something precious that we have at the
moment and something that I believe is a gift we have
to offer the whole church. For at present we have a
process whereby we can all live together. Yes! I know
at times not easily, but we have shown the rest of the
church a unique way to live where there is serious
disagreement on a fundamental issue.....but let us not

lose this high degree of unity we still have in this period of reception of women in the priesthood, because, and we have to be clear about this, the reception period will have to come to an end with the consecration of the first woman bishop. There cannot be a time of reception of women into the episcopate because there cannot be anything provisional about the episcopate.'

After I retired, a way forward for members of The Society of St. Wilfrid and St. Hilda and other traditionalists was identified in the House of Bishops 'Declaration', which came into force in November 2014. In view of the nature of the Church of England, and the serious conversations among ourselves and with other ecumenical partners over forty years, I believe 'The Bishops' Declaration' and its Statement of 'Five Guiding Principles' was the most satisfactory outcome possible. Catholics have something they can live with, while remaining in, and very much part of, the Church of England. In December 2014, Bishop Tony Robinson, Bishop of Wakefield, Chairman of Forward in Faith, wrote:

In the Declaration, the House of Bishops has invited us to flourish within the Church of England's life and structures. Parishes should pass a resolution under the Declaration not as a means of distancing themselves from the rest of the Church of England, but as a response to the invitation to flourish within it.

While the Society provides support more widely, the number of parishes that have actually passed the

'Declaration' now exceeds 425, and there are eight serving bishops and eleven actively retired bishops who are members of The Society. In retirement, I minister wherever I am sent or invited; but my base is in a parish of The Society. I have been encouraged by my experience both of my home parish and of the many Society parishes I have visited in recent years. Inevitably, a large number of those parishes are in areas of great deprivation, ministering sacrificially to the whole community. They need real support - prayerful and material - from us all.

I am pleased that most of my responsibilities outside the Diocese of Blackburn were of a pastoral nature. My interest in the Healing Ministry began when, as a sixth-form student, I met the chaplain to Dorothy Kerin (1889-1963), the founder of Burrswood Christian Hospital and Place of Healing on the Kent and Sussex border, which I have visited from time to time over some fifty-five years. When I became a bishop, I was already President of the Crowhurst Christian Healing Centre, which is located in my previous archdeaconry. So, I was pleased to be invited to represent the House of Bishops on the Healing Ministry Steering Group.

By the time I joined it, the Steering Group had produced the report *A Time to Heal* (Archbishops' Council, 2000, London, CHP) which had been warmly received in the General Synod and widely disseminated in the Church of England and throughout the Anglican Communion. The group had been responsible for other impressive publications, presentations and conferences - often working with ecumenical partners. The healing ministry was becoming more central to the life of the Church - indeed, one motive for preaching on the healing ministry at my first Diocesan Clergy Conference, in 2004, was to send out a clear signal that the ministry of healing is a normal part of the ministry of the diocese.

The Revd Beatrice Brandon was the convener of the steering group; a couple of years after I joined, she confirmed the general feeling, which I shared, that the group, in its existing form, was nearing the end of its useful life. We went to see Chris Smith, the Chief of Staff to the Archbishop of Canterbury, initiating the process which led to Beatrice becoming the Archbishops' Adviser, meeting regularly with me, as lead bishop for the healing ministry. Beatrice was blessed with great energy and enthusiasm, organising national conferences and setting up 'workshops'; she also made presentations to theological colleges, diocesan synods and more widely. Beatrice had also started researching into and working on the deliverance ministry. This is an area of ministry with which I had had little involvement, so I asked Beatrice to work as closely as possible with Bishop Dominic Walker, OGS, then Bishop of Monmouth. The House of Bishops' Steering Committee had agreed that Beatrice should work with all dioceses, collating and analysing deliverance ministry survey data. She also researched this ministry across twenty-nine denominations in Churches Together in England. It was a great joy, shortly before I retired, that Beatrice was awarded the

Lambeth degree of Doctor of Divinity, for her extensive research, and in recognition of her contribution to the healing ministry. She was the first woman priest to be awarded a Lambeth DD.

I have been critical elsewhere about the tendency of the Church to under-fund work that it believes to be important, even when it commissions it. If we were to lose the colossal army of volunteers, sometimes undertaking very skilled work, upon which we depend in so many areas of activity, we would be in an 'apocalyptic' situation. Without the generosity of the Beatrice Brandon Trust, the funding provided by the Church alone would have covered little more than the resources required for a few meetings of our group each year. The Church should perhaps be less ambitious and more modest in what it undertakes - doing what it does undertake very well and funding it adequately.

An impressive conference for the Diocesan Healing Advisers was organised at Church House, Westminster in 2011. I was invited to speak on the theme of the healing ministry in the New Testament. I approached the subject under four headings: thanksgiving, reconciliation, fullness of life and good news. In that address, I summarised my understanding of the healing ministry in the Church - starting with thanksgiving, for as we look back on our lives, our prayer must surely be, 'Thanks be to God'. According to Meister Eckhart, the German Dominican mystic (1260-1327), 'If the only prayer people said in the whole of their life was "thank you" they would have prayed well'. In considering our calling to live the new and full life of reconciliation, I said: 'Here I believe we need to be careful and to distinguish between curing, which means restoring function, and healing as the bringing of wholeness and soundness to any or every aspect of human life. Many people with disabilities, and surely all of us with our defects, believe that God's purpose is to refine us and bring us to maturity through our afflictions. We cannot assume that a cure is always desirable or right. As someone with a disability put it to me, "People see me as an eight-cylinder engine firing on six cylinders, but they are actually wrong. I am a six-cylinder engine firing on all six cylinders." ' I ended the talk by quoting first from the report *A Time to Heal,* 'When God heals it is a sign that true mission extends not only to spiritual needs but also to the transformation of society and ultimately the healing of creation itself. Just as all history finds its true meaning and fulfilment in Jesus, and just as the Father's plan from the beginning has been to unify and reconcile everything in Jesus, so too the Father's plan is and always has been to unify and reconcile everything in our lives to Jesus. Thanksgiving, Reconciliation, Fullness of Life and Proclamation of the Good News is the way we co-operate with Jesus as we bring everything under His Lordship and look to His total healing as all things are consummated in Him.'

Shortly after I took on the healing ministry responsibility, I was honoured to be asked to succeed Bishop Jack Nicholls, Bishop of Sheffield (1997-

2008) as Warden of the Guild of St. Raphael, another healing-ministry post. The Guild, founded in 1915, is dedicated to extending the Lord's ministry of healing - particularly through the sacraments of healing. In recent years, the Guild has been blessed with extremely able and energetic Sub-Wardens, one of whom was Canon Paul Nener, Vicar of St. John's Tuebrook, Liverpool (1995-2010), a very distinguished consultant surgeon in his earlier working life. In retirement he became the Guild's Roving Ambassador, and was succeeded as Sub-Warden by Canon Rodney Middleton, a priest with wide experience of the healing ministry, who had been Vicar of St. James', Haydock since 1995.

The annual meeting of the Guild was always keenly supported, and took place in parts of the country where the Guild was particularly active. One of my very last acts as Bishop of Blackburn was to preside and preach at the 2012 annual meeting, which was at Liverpool Cathedral. Three years after I left the diocese, the Guild celebrated the centenary of its independent life as a Guild. (It had split from the Guild of Health to allow the two groups to concentrate on different aspects of the ministry of healing - appropriately, on the day of their centenaries, the guilds were to reunite, to become once more a single organisation.)

It was another privilege to be asked to succeed Bishop Jack Nicholls as Chair of the Committee for Ministry of and Among Deaf and Disabled People (CMDDP), which was one of the sub-committees of the Archbishops' Council. The Revd. Philip Maddock had been the Adviser to the CMDDP for some three years when I joined the committee, and I much enjoyed working with him and the elected committee. The brief was to support and to encourage the ministries of deaf people, of people with disabilities, and of all those who work with them.

The committee was lively, committed, and achieved a great deal. While it worked satisfactorily as the 'Deaf and Disabled' Committee, I am not sure ministry to the deaf sits appropriately with ministry to the disabled; nevertheless, we managed to address issues of importance to both groups. With approximately nineteen percent of the population in the UK suffering from hearing loss - and, among those, the majority are hard-of-hearing rather than deaf - and some twenty percent of the population suffering from some form of general disability, it is a shame that the Church could not see this ministry as a greater priority.

When Philip Maddock and I were approaching retirement, we set up a sub-committee under our vice-Chair, Cherry Vann, Archdeacon of Rochdale, to find ways of taking forward the work of the committee. I was disappointed that the best response that the Archbishops' Council could offer was a limited budget for a very part-time post to succeed Philip. As I said in a speech in the House of Lords concerning a Government Spending Review, 'If the level of civilisation of a society is judged by the way it treats its most vulnerable people, then in the light of the spending review it is time for us take stock of where we are in our society'. If we are prepared to criticise the government for introducing some cuts for the disabled, we should not be doing anything similar in the church.

While funding for the deaf and disabled may not have been a priority for the Synod, it was an achievement to secure a prominent place in the Synod during its meetings for deaf people and their signers; they were brought to the front and seated to the side of the bishops with their signer. One other success was the report, jointly produced by CMDDP and the Mission and Public Affairs Division, *Opening the Doors-Ministry with People with Learning Disabilities and on the Autistic Spectrum,* which I presented to the Synod. It was warmly received and widely studied in the church.

I was also a member, for some time, of the Urban Bishops' Panel, under the chairmanship of the Bishop of Ripon and Leeds, Bishop John Packer. The two of us also held the Urban Issues brief jointly in the House of Lords in my final two years. I also served on the Senior Appointments Group (Episcopal). There were other *ad hoc* committees and meetings to attend, most of which took place in London – the staff on the Virgin Pendolino Class 390 from Preston to Euston often said to me, 'Oh! It's you again.' I also held a few north-west responsibilities. I sometimes felt that I had too many outside duties, but in comparison with the load carried by some of my fellow bishops, I was fortunate.

After I went into the House of Lords, my travel to London increased further. Twenty-six bishops sit in the House of Lords. Of the forty-four diocesan bishops in the Church of England, two are ineligible to sit in the House, the Bishop in Europe, and the Bishop of Sodor and Man, who sits in the Tynwald. The two Archbishops go into the Lords on appointment, as do the Bishops of London, Durham and Winchester. Therefore, twenty-one of the thirty-seven eligible bishops take up the remaining seats, and they are allocated on seniority by length of service. Generally, this means a bishop will go into the House after about four years, although I had to wait some five-and-a-half years. While we are a distinctive group, we do not have a whip, and we do not always vote the same way; we do not align ourselves to any political party and we do not attend meetings of other political parties, except, at our personal discretion, Crossbencher meetings. There is always a duty bishop in the Lords, who starts the working day by leading the prayers. Both Houses of Parliament begin with prayer. If it was the end of the week, some Noble Lords, particularly from Lancashire, would ask me if I would read Psalm 121, 'I will lift up mine eyes unto the hills'. Bishops are usually 'duty bishop' for three weeks a year but are also expected to attend as frequently as their other duties permit. Bishops do not speak just on religious issues, but on a wide range of subjects that come before the House. God is not God of the Church alone: it is His world, and we are called to engage in it at a deep level.

During half of my time in the House there was a Labour

government, and, for the other half, the Conservative-
led coalition. When there is a change of government,
the bishops do not change their seats, as they always
sit on the bishops' bench on the government side of
The House. For most of my time, the convener of
the bishops in the Lords was the Bishop of Leicester,
Bishop Tim Stevens. We were allocated portfolios,
and the bishops holding the relevant portfolio would
be in the Chamber when matters relating to their areas
of responsibility were being debated, or, at least, brief
the duty bishop, who would speak on their behalf. All
bishops are free to speak on any subject, to submit
questions, and to ask supplementary questions at every
Question Time. In most cases, when a Lord Spiritual
rises to ask a supplementary, and another peer also
rises, the House will defer to the bishop. It is only
on special occasions, such as the State Opening of
Parliament, that all peers wear their distinctive dress;
but the bishops have always worn the black chimere,
black scarf and white rochet in the chamber and in the
division lobby.

*2011. President Obama shaking hands with the
Bishop of Blackburn.*

This does mean it can be seen quite clearly which lobby they are going through. I recall on the day after the government lost a vote by a single vote, Bishop Tim Stevens told me that the Leader of the House had told him that I was the cause of the motion being lost, by going through the 'Not Content' division lobby. Bishop Tim did point out that there were some two hundred others who went through the same lobby.

House of Lords. Adult Education debate.

Unlike at the General Synod, if a bishop is on the list to speak, they will always take their turn, just like every other peer. The House is self-regulating, and members simply stand, when the previous speaker on the list has finished. I spoke on a wide range of subjects, and always tried to be present if there was any business relating to Lancashire and welfare reform and poverty. It was good to speak sometimes on subjects that I would not normally choose, such as the digital economy bill. I thought I would be very nervous about making my maiden speech - on transport - but felt at ease as soon as I stood up to speak. Lord Adonis, the Secretary of State for Transport, was on the front bench and immediately sent a warm and appreciative note to me, and I received an equally warm letter from the Lord Speaker, Baroness Hayman.

By convention, the peer who speaks immediately after a maiden speech congratulates the new Peer or Lord Spiritual, and I was delighted that was Lord Judd of Portsea, who sat almost directly behind me, and was a keen church member. Frank Judd is a former Director of OXFAM, and I have always had the highest regard for him. My particular interest in the political life of our nation goes back to when I was at school, and to when I read politics in my first year at University. It was therefore pleasing to have someone speaking about me who first went into Parliament around about that time. Frank became an MP in 1966, and later served in the governments of Harold Wilson and of James Callaghan.

I found government ministers and shadow ministers generally willing to meet bishops and to talk about particular issues. While I am aware that there are some who see little purpose in having bishops in the House in the twenty-first century, I never encountered anything other than support for what we did. There was a general understanding that we were involved in the life of the communities in our dioceses and thus had much to bring to the House.

When I am invited to speak to groups and organisations, I am frequently asked to say something about meeting the Queen. A new diocesan bishop pays homage to Her Majesty the Queen at Buckingham Palace, usually being presented by the Lord Chancellor. In conversation with the Queen after the ceremony, I was delighted to find out how much she knew about my new diocese, even though at that time my cathedral was one of the few she had not visited. As mentioned earlier, Her Majesty came to Blackburn in my time, but did not visit the cathedral for the Maundy Service until two years after I had left. The Queen kindly invites bishops to one of her garden parties every year, and there are other occasions, usually when she is visiting the diocese, when the bishop will meet her or other members of the Royal Family. Perhaps the most special occasion is when one's turn comes to preach at Sandringham shortly after Christmas - which usually occurs only once in each episcopal appointment.

Returning to breakfast after celebrating 8.00am Eucharist at Sandringham Parish Church.

I much enjoyed my stay at Sandringham, and joined part of a weekend house party. I arrived on the Saturday for dinner, celebrated the eight o'clock Eucharist on Sunday morning at Sandringham Parish Church, and was greeted by all the Queen's corgis as I walked back from church in the snow. I then preached at Matins, and joined the house party for lunch, followed by a visit around the estate, including the stables, and had tea with the congregation of the parish church at the Rectory.

At dinner on Sunday, only the Queen, the Duke of Edinburgh, the Equerry, the Lady-in-Waiting, and the visiting bishop are present. This is, of course, a very special time, and included some discussion of the sermon. The Queen and the Duke were most generous with the amount of time they gave to me, and I have many happy memories of that weekend. As a child we lived just a few miles from Sandringham at RAF Bircham Newton, where, the Duke informed me, he learnt to fly helicopters. In those days we frequently visited the Sandringham Estate and I remember my sister saying she wondered what it would be like behind the front door we used to gaze at. I was pleased to be able to inform her fifty years later.

Bishops are away from their dioceses on other duties a great deal, but the only time I was absent for as long as three weeks was during the Lambeth Conference, in 2008. Since 1867, and generally at ten-yearly intervals, all bishops of the world-wide Anglican Communion have been invited by the Archbishop of Canterbury to come together, initially at Lambeth, and, since 1978, at the University of Kent, Canterbury. In more recent years, bishops' spouses have also been invited, with some sessions shared with bishops, but also separate programmes.

Sadly, because of the nature of some of the issues facing the Communion, and the decisions a few provinces had made with regard to them, a small but significant number felt unable to join the rest of the Communion for this Conference. I regretted that some personal friends were among those who could not attend, and I had some sympathy for certain of their concerns about the direction of travel of parts of the Communion. Before the Conference began, each diocese extended hospitality to a small number of overseas bishops over a long weekend, and, in Blackburn, we greatly enjoyed the visit of three bishops and their wives.

It is important to remember that each part of the Anglican Communion is governed by its own Bishops in Synod; consequently, the Lambeth Conference in no way constitutes an executive body imposing doctrine and discipline. While the Archbishop of Canterbury is President of the Lambeth Conference – rather than an Anglican 'Pope' - the Conference is the place in which the bishops of the Communion express their minds on controversial matters and other issues. (It is reckoned that, during the thirteen Lambeth Conferences, seven hundred-and-fifty issues have been addressed.) While we all knew that there were growing tensions in the Communion to be faced, the way in which the conference was structured helped us to face them. We started with a three-day retreat in Canterbury Cathedral, with addresses by Archbishop Rowan. This, for me and for many others, was the 'jewel' of the Conference. Indeed, the whole Conference was centred around the Eucharist and Evening Prayer, and there was a special 'prayer centre' at the heart of the Conference - mainly for silent prayer - staffed by the chaplaincy team.

Christine and I met so many inspirational people. One bishop to whom we spoke lived in constant fear of the Taliban. Another bishop's wife had bravely stood up to a sustained attack from rebels in Sierra Leone. Many lived in abject poverty. I remember some Zimbabweans being amazed at the quantity of food on our tables. Not surprisingly, there was a huge divide between the attitude of those from the developed nations and those from the developing nations. Some of the most inspirational people and some of the excellent contributions to the Conference came from leaders and representatives of other denominations - and the evening with the Chief Rabbi was one of the highlights.

Among the other important features of the Conference was the daily bible study with groups of some eight to ten bishops; these provided a most enriching experience of sharing and of prayer. I was the only bishop in my group whose first language was English. The main discussion groups employed a form of *indaba*, a decision-making process used particularly in Africa. It is based on real listening to each other, enabling each bishop to speak what was on his heart, and providing assurance that others would listen with respect. Sometimes it proved to be difficult, but undoubtedly engendered a spirit of constructive dialogue and deepened our commitment to each other. I can recall a tense, but respectful, discussion about gay marriage - which one American bishop favoured and another, from Africa, totally opposed. Those present were moved when the American bishop said he promised to reflect prayerfully and with great care on all that the African bishop had said before he made a final decision on the matter in his Synod. That small - perhaps not so small - response and gesture filled me with great hope. Maybe we had been changed by the *indaba*? I suppose the test would come, as with so many conferences, when we returned home. Would it be back to business as usual?

I have said little about the main theme of the conference,' Equipping Bishops for God's Mission'. Following various mission initiatives stretching back to the Decade of Evangelism, the Church in England might have felt growing confidence that progress was being made with its own growth strategies (including the mission action planning in Blackburn); however, the opportunity provided by the conference to look at the life of the Church in several other parts of the world proved salutary. I came away with the strong impression that bishops from the developing parts of the Communion were living and engaging most deeply in God's Mission to His world.

I felt fortunate that a Lambeth Conference occurred during my time at Blackburn. I wish I had maintained contact with those bishops I had got to know best during the three-week conference. I am still very hopeful for parts of the Anglican Communion as we move further into the twenty-first century; however, since Lambeth 2008, there has been a disappointing willingness on the part of some provinces to take decisions without listening to the rest of the Anglican Communion. That approach, I believe, could lead to our becoming *de facto* an Anglican Federation, which is very different from being the Anglican Communion.

I pray that when provinces are tempted to set fire to much of what has been handed down by and to the Church, they will think carefully of the whole Communion. If the changes they propose are designed to make them more relevant to their local cultures, they should consider what the evidence suggests. The advancement of more secular thinking in the church brings little or no positive results – indeed, mostly negative outcomes. It is surely wiser to remember, as a fellow bishop reminded me recently, that it is not we who interrogate the great tradition of which we are part, but the great tradition that interrogates us.

12 LEAVING THE SEE - Blackburn (4)

Christine, my wife, has been with me throughout the whole of my ministry. For nearly all of that time she was teaching Religious Studies, mostly at 'A' level. She loved it - especially her more than twenty years at Mayfield Convent School in East Sussex. We had never been a 'joint ministry couple', and Christine has always responded to her vocation to teach and her own informal ministry of service, encouragement and hospitality in the parish. We did face something of a dilemma over the move to Blackburn; for we both felt that the demands of the post would require all hands to the pump.

Christine, most generously, gave up her final years of teaching, but said she was not just going to be a camp follower. She much enjoyed being in the parishes, and would always come with me at least once on a Sunday and very often during the week. The days when Bishop's House came with a large staff had long since gone; we both undertook the routine tasks that were required around the house. Although we had help with special occasions, much of Christine's time was taken up with seemingly endless catering, entertaining and 'estate management'.

Christine had her own informal pastoral ministry, which was appreciated everywhere we served. She had the gift of seeing possible openings and gaps, and responding to them; and, also, of reassuring and supporting people. Whenever I arrived in a parish in the diocese without her, there was disappointment. I would like to mention just three areas among many, in which Christine made a special contribution to the life of the diocese. The Mothers' Union (MU) provided a means for Christine to engage independently with the parishes. The Blackburn Diocesan Mothers' Union had the largest membership outside Africa; indeed, the special link between the Dioceses of Blackburn and of the Free State (previously Bloemfontein) – the oldest such link in the Anglican Communion - began as a Mothers' Union link. We had two excellent MU presidents during our time in the diocese, Marion Whitehead and then Beverley Laycock, and they became Christine's good friends. We were amazed by the number and size of the MU branches. In many parishes, the MU was playing a key role, particularly in social issues such as child poverty and violence against women. The organisation represents an important voice in upholding Christian family values throughout the country. Christine enjoyed supporting many of its diocesan initiatives, particularly those focused on areas of deprivation, students, and prisons. The MU also sponsored an 'Away from it All' scheme, providing breaks for families facing difficulties, which had a caravan at its disposal. Christine had a great time visiting MU branches, giving talks and speaking at deanery festivals.

Sunflower House – a hospice for children with Aids-related illnesses in Bloemfontein - was another project close to Christine's heart. She was a trustee, and always counted it a privilege to give talks to raise funds for this work. In speaking about her two visits to Sunflower House, she said, 'It was the children who found me, and it was a life-changing experience.'

By the early years of the new millennium it had become difficult to know what arrangements to make for clergy spouses; these were changing times, and ministry to spouses around the diocese was mainly informal. This made it important to ensure that everyone had the possibility of support. Christine consulted the deaneries for ideas about centrally-organised provision - and an overwhelming majority did not want too many demands made of them.

Granddaughter Millie fascinated by the mitre, 2011.

It was decided therefore to have just one event at Bishop's House each year. When asked how to set about renewing the church, one bishop said, 'more prayer and more parties'. So, one year there would be an 'Adventure in Prayer' day, with worship, prayer workshops, and a leisurely lunch; the next, a 'Spouses' Supper' with the emphasis on fun - appealing particularly to the younger contingent. The occasions were enjoyable, with the social interaction as the most valuable element.

Those who know me at all, will be aware of how much I owe to Christine, to our daughter Claire, her husband Walter Featherstone - whom she married just after we started at Blackburn - and, later on, our two granddaughters, Millie and Isabelle. They have all been a huge support, ensuring I have maintained some level of normality. It is a real joy to be able to spend more time with them in retirement.

In the last issue of *The See* to appear before we left the diocese, the following comment was made under the heading 'Mission Action Planning'. 'Mission has been at the heart of Bishop Nicholas' time in the Blackburn Diocese as he has encouraged others to share their faith, "grow in holiness", "be the Church better", and "come and see". All mission is God's mission, and we always need to remember that His mission does not begin with us, but actually in His heart. We do not initiate mission, neither will we consummate it. Our calling is simply to engage in His mission to His world. We are called to share our faith, to bear witness to the promise of Christ, and to lead others to faith; and it is the Holy Spirit who is the principal agent in our work.' 'Mission Action Planning' and its successor, 'Going for Growth', occupied much of our time, and may be regarded as two of the documents particularly associated with my episcopate. I did also emphasise that the Burnley Report, 'The Shape of Things to Come – Foundations for Mission and Ministry' should be read alongside 'Going for Growth'. 'The Shape of Things to Come' was published shortly before I left. An immense amount of detailed and careful work was put into this impressive report, with the task force chaired by Bishop John Goddard, Bishop of Burnley, and three working groups: Theology, Ministry and Deanery. Its findings were not prescriptive, but it included sound recommendations to prepare the diocese to meet the challenges it would be facing in 2020.

My successor, Bishop Julian Henderson, has lengthened the process to 2026, the centenary of the creation of the diocese; at the same time, 'Going for Growth' and 'The Shape of Things to Come' have been incorporated into 'Vision 2026'. It is an encouragement to feel that some of what went into these projects will continue to be part of the life of the diocese as it grows towards its centenary, and as we continue to support it with our prayer.

I had completed the required thirty-seven years for a full pension in 2010, so I decided I would retire at the end of 2012, after I had celebrated my sixty-sixth birthday. This also meant that I had served successively for thirty years as rural/area dean (in some dioceses they are called rural and in some area) of two deaneries, archdeacon, and bishop. I was beginning to feel that the time was approaching when I ought to change the extreme-performance-versatile tyres I had been driving with for so long, for a simple performance set.

Towards the end of 2012 seemed to be a good time to bid farewell to the diocese. Bishop John of Burnley, who was a year younger than me, was beginning to think of retiring, and, with his long experience as a bishop and his wisdom and energy, he would become 'acting diocesan' during the vacancy. Archdeacon John of Blackburn was also looking towards retirement, and Christopher, the Dean of Blackburn, again a year younger than me, was staying on to see the new build at the cathedral through. While I would have liked to have completed a full ten years in the see, my departure at that time meant that my successor could make these senior appointments at the outset of his episcopate.

Every year brings some tricky situations, but in my final year there were a number of very difficult problems: a few complaints were made under the Clergy Discipline Measure 2003 (CDM), including against me. It would be wrong to write about the complaints that concerned others; and I have already referred to this 'new' disciplinary measure in the church. However, as mentioned earlier, one of the complaints against me was issued by Chichester Diocese, in which I had served previously for twenty-two years. The Archbishop of York, in his adjudication of the complaint against my part in this case, accepted the preliminary scrutiny report of the Provincial Registrar of the Province of

York - that I had done all that I was required to do - and he dismissed the complaint. The complainants accepted the judgement, and did not request a review of the Archbishop's decision by Lord Justice Mummery, the President of Tribunals. Over six years later, despite the dismissal, it inevitably came up again, when I was asked to submit a witness statement to, and to give evidence before, the Independent Inquiry into Child Sexual Abuse.

I have mentioned this case for three reasons - first, because it took seven months for a decision to be made. I was pleased to have received the archbishop's judgement   just days before my farewell service in the cathedral. Others have had to wait longer, and the length of wait is unacceptable. Certainly, I acknowledge that this is as nothing compared to what those who have been abused have suffered.

Secondly, although the number of clergy in the church who have committed such abuse is tiny, as I have said earlier, we are deeply ashamed that any abuse has happened - even one case would be totally unacceptable. It is therefore worth noting the progress made of late by the Church, in company with other agencies, with major developments in child protection and safeguarding policies.

Thirdly, however brief and sketchy an account of a ministry in the Church of England in the late-twentieth and early twenty-first centuries may be, it would be seriously lacking if it failed to acknowledge that one of the major failings of the world-wide Church has been in what we now call safeguarding: our inability to listen to, or to believe, those who came forward. Some years after I left the Diocese of Chichester, following a report by Baroness Butler-Sloss, a number of historic cases surfaced, and a few priests went to prison, including the priest who was the cause of the CDM taken out against me. I know that many other organisations have failed or fallen short in their care of children, and faced, and continue to face, allegations of child abuse; but what is so shameful for the Church is that it must be a place in which children and all vulnerable people are always secure and loved.

It is difficult to understand how this happened - especially as there can be no excuses. Before the greatly-improved training came about, we understood little about child abuse. Most people did not realise that it was an addiction and, therefore, that there is a strong probability of re-offending. Some in authority invariably believed the clergy, as a matter of form. The distinction between a pastoral matter and what is now called a safeguarding issue was not grasped. Many would possibly echo what Cardinal Cormac Murphy O'Connor wrote in *An English Spring* (Bloomsbury 2015), referring to the problems in the Roman Catholic Church: 'I'd been foolish and naive and, perhaps I had drifted into that little space where kindness blurs into weakness.'

It was a privilege working with the Safeguarding Team in Blackburn, which was led during most of my time by Nancy Talbot; the process improved, greatly assisted by the new policies which came through from the House of Bishops. It represents a major step forward that the Church no longer works alone. For many years now, we have learned to work in a multi-disciplinary way: the moment an issue arises, the relevant agencies, including the police and the local authority designated officer, are called together with the church safeguarding officer and the bishop or his representative. I truly believe that I did 'what I was required to do' all those years ago, in early 1997 but it fell short and I deeply regret that. I know the matter would have been handled very much more satisfactorily in recent times, by the diocese, the police, to whom the complaint was made, and other agencies.

I much enjoyed my final months, discharging my episcopal duties right to the end. By chance, this last period of service included the Preston Guild Festival (founded in 1179) which takes place only once every twenty years ('once in a Preston Guild' is a common saying in Lancashire). These days, this is a multi-cultural event; the churches, as well as being involved in other events, have their own programme, including a special service in Avenham Park. Archbishop Sentamu took part in the divine service at Preston Minster in the morning and Cardinal Nichols, Archbishop of Westminster, was able to join us for the Ecumenical Service in the park – as well as Aled Jones. I felt especially honoured to attend the Guild Service and give the Blessing.

For my last bishop's staff meeting we visited the House

of the Resurrection at Mirfield, where I had received my initial priestly formation. During my ministry in the north-west I had returned to Mirfield to make my confession and to receive spiritual direction; I had also made my pre-consecration retreat there and returned every year for my annual retreat. I have been a Priest Companion of the Fraternity of the Resurrection for many years, owing much to the Community. After our staff meeting in the retreat house, we joined the community for the midday Office, Mass and lunch, followed by a conducted tour around the redesigned and restored community church. Since liturgy and worship were at the heart of our life as a diocese, it seemed right to take leave of my colleagues in such a special church, designed for liturgical excellence.

In the evening, the staff, with their spouses, gave us a magnificent dinner at Whalley Abbey. As always, Christine Nelson, the Manager, and her team had provided excellent hospitality. Later, at the final Diocesan Synod, Archdeacon John Hawley and a small team created a specially-prepared tribute on a compact disc - and I found it difficult to recognise myself in what was being said. There were also warm tributes to Christine on the CD. Because the recorded tribute at the Diocesan Synod was such a well-kept secret (with even the Archbishop of York being interviewed about my ministry), when I asked Christine if she would like to come to my final Synod, she said she had never been to one so far and did not intend to start with my last one.

Christine was present, of course, at my final Eucharist in the cathedral, which was in celebration of Christ the King, and in thanksgiving for the diocese, the County of Lancashire, and my ministry as their bishop. The cathedral offered a wonderful service, with the cathedral choir and the cathedral girls' choir under Samuel Hudson, the director of music. The setting for the Eucharist was Schubert's Mass in G, with two trumpeters from the Northern Chamber Orchestra. I was really delighted that those represented in the congregation included local schools, parishes from throughout the diocese, parishes I had served throughout my ministry, and those with whom I had worked. I was keen that we should have a musical contribution from children and young people from the diocese, under the direction of Sue Witts, our assistant director of education. During the service, I presented the one-hundredth 'Child Friendly Church' award (we were the first diocese to reach that number). Both the many gifts we received, and the speeches - particularly from my suffragans, Bishop John Goddard and Bishop Geoff Pearson - were far too generous. I was glad to be invited back to Blackburn when they retired, to pay tribute to them as colleagues and good friends, and for their wider contribution to the diocese during my episcopate.

The service ended with me laying down the diocesan bishop's crosier which I had taken up at my installation while the choir sang C.H.H. Parry's 'I was glad'. I then gave the dismissal, and walked out with Christine. As I left the chancel, the Principal of St. Wilfred's

Academy in Blackburn handed me a pastoral staff that the Academy had made for my personal use, and which I carry frequently in my retirement ministry.

At the Altar at my final Eucharist in the Cathedral with the two suffragan bishops

My retirement from the See was still not quite final. There remained a few commitments and farewells. Perhaps it was not inappropriate that my last public engagement should be to celebrate the Eucharist and preach in Liverpool Cathedral, at the annual meeting of the Guild of St. Raphael, of which I was still the warden.

The Blackburn years were very full, a time of considerable change, with much emphasis on mission and evangelism. I sometimes wonder if we tried to do too much. I recall the words of Cosmo Lang (1864-1945) who had been successively Bishop of Stepney,

Archbishop of York, and Archbishop of Canterbury: 'I look back on my time as Bishop and Archbishop and think of all the hopes and plans for which I began, and now, at the end what? Certainly, there was enough and to spare of doing, yet after all the ceaseless process of doing, what was actually done? A church life somewhat encouraged and invigorated, I hope, but how many souls were brought nearer to God by all this doing? The words of the Methodist hymn come to mind 'doing is a deadly thing'. What is certain is that much more of true value might have been borne if I had cared less for doing and more for being. If the inner life had been kept more true, the outer life would have borne more fruit.'

Laying down the Staff

Looking back at my time in Blackburn, I recall that I often did emphasise, particularly in my addresses to clergy and at the annual Chrism Eucharist the need for faithfulness to the daily Office, and for our time with holy scripture and for adoring Our Lord in the Blessed Sacrament, and just being with Him. And yet Archbishop Cosmo's words still give pause for reflection.

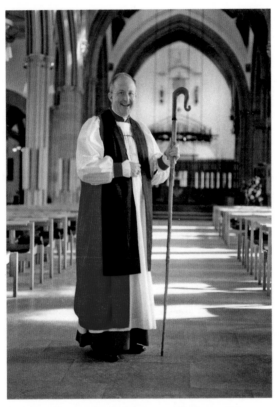

The official portriat which hangs with those of the seven previous Bishops of Blackburn.

13   BACK TO THE SEA. RETIREMENT

We purchased a house in Bexhill-on-Sea two years before I retired. Although Bexhill was within the archdeaconry in which I had previously served, that was nine years earlier, and I had not worked in any other capacity in Bexhill deanery. The diocese had undergone much change: Bishop John Hind had retired as the diocesan bishop; both suffragan bishops had left the diocese, and many familiar faces were no longer present. Bishop Martin Warner, formerly Suffragan Bishop of Whitby, was now the Bishop of Chichester. I have liked and admired Bishop Martin, since his days as Priest-Administrator at the Shrine of Our Lady of Walsingham (1993-2003). He has always been generous and hospitable, involving his retired bishops in many ways. Bishop Martin, with his own staff team, has increased the pace of change begun by Bishop John Hind, addressing with great focus and determination many of the problems faced by the church and the diocese as we move further into the twenty-first century. With his safeguarding team, he has drawn on the work of the enquiries commissioned by his predecessor, and tackled the historic cases which surfaced in his early years. He has opened them to the legal and judicial system, while ensuring that the safeguarding provisions of the Diocese of Chichester constitute an example of excellent practice in the Church of England.

I was confident, therefore, that I would be remembered by very few, except perhaps at All Saints' Sidley. In the event, rather a lot of people turned out to have long memories. It was a great joy to move into our own house - as first-time buyers. It was also a joy to return to All Saints', as T.S. Eliot wrote 'in my beginning is my end' (East Coker). I had known All Saints' since 1957, and as a boy of ten my faith was nurtured there so it appeared to be the ideal retirement location.

However, the first few months of retirement in Bexhill proved to be far from easy - it was a time for re-adjusting and getting settled into our new home. I received the bishop's Permission to Officiate at Easter 2013, and the Bishop in Europe made me an Honorary Assistant Bishop in his diocese at that time; and it was good to return to ministry, at All Saints' and other churches I had known previously. The following Advent, the Bishop of Chichester made me an Honorary Assistant Bishop, in company with two other colleagues who had just retired, Bishop Geoffrey Rowell (former Bishop in Europe) and Bishop Michael Langrish (former Bishop of Exeter).

All Saints' displayed great generosity when it came to the fortieth anniversary of my ordination to the priesthood, at which I concelebrated Mass with three former Diocesan Bishops, namely John Hind (Chichester), Geoffrey Rowell, and Michael Langrish, with the Bishop Suffragan of Horsham (representing the Diocesan Bishop) presiding from the Episcopal Throne. My longest-serving chaplain, Fr. David Arnold, preached, and Suzanne Parrott, the sacristan, produced one of her very fine buffets. The collection supported the refurbishment of the former choir vestry, which is now the community room.

All Saints' has always been the prominent Anglo-Catholic Church in the Bexhill area; its tradition has never been an issue, and is unchallenged. It is a community church: outreach to the surrounding estates and other parishes happens naturally and is not just talked about. The church is in the middle of the community, accepted as God's Church by churchgoing and non-churchgoing parishioners alike. They all know that it is there to serve them, to care for them, and to pray for them, particularly through the daily Mass. The church hall effectively serves as a community centre: the church keenly supports its uniformed organisations, and holds many social functions, including an annual pantomime. It is a tough parish, in an economically-deprived area, but the people there are generous-hearted and very hard working.

The present parish priest, Father Michael Bailey, an Irishman, and a former senior cancer nurse, has developed the mission of the parish considerably, and is very generous to his retired clergy. In addition, Fr. Michael has assumed responsibility for a town-centre parish, and for the training of a curate. It is fortunate that he has an insatiable appetite for work.

Shortly before I retired, my spiritual director mentioned that quite a few people find they run into health issues after retirement. I laughed. However, after seven months in Bexhill, I walked through the doors of The Conquest Hospital, Hastings, for the first time since that final hospital chaplains' meeting shortly before my consecration as Bishop of Blackburn. I was about to be discharged from a Urology Clinic at Bexhill Hospital; however, the specialist registrar in charge of the clinic voiced residual concerns over the symptoms that had led me to seek medical advice initially – despite being apparently symptom free on the current assessment. He therefore ordered a full examination under local anaesthetic; I later realised that I probably owe my life to that registrar.

Helen Teixeira, the specialist registrar who performed the full examination, helpfully turned the screen towards me, and I immediately realised that all was not well. I was due to go to Rome for a conference the following week, and on the last day we were to be presented to the Pope, at the conclusion to the weekly general audience. Helen was a young Roman Catholic, and very excited by the changes Pope Francis was bringing about - she told the consultant we must delay the surgery.

I had not had a surgical operation since I was fourteen, but after having done much work over the years in hospitals, it was good to have the experience of being a patient. The anaesthetists had a hearty laugh when I told them that the day of the operation was in fact World Toilet Day - a good day, surely, on which to have urological surgery. Habit in prayer is an excellent discipline. I came out of theatre; the clock was coming up to 12 noon and my first words were to tell the nurse it was time for the Angelus – the memorial of the Incarnation. Shortly after I returned to the ward I had a sandwich lunch, during which I was visited by the senior chaplain, a Roman Catholic in the Ordinariate of Our Lady of Walsingham. Indeed, as Archdeacon, I had presented him to the Bishop for ordination as a priest of God for service in the Church of England. Half-way through my sandwich he told me how short-staffed they were in the chaplaincy and invited me to help them out when I recovered, which I thought was fine timing!

Ten days after the resection, I returned to see the consultant, who informed me that the histology indicated a high-grade cancer in the bladder. They would need to remove the whole of the bladder and prostate and fix me up with a urostomy – but I would still be able to ride my bicycle. While many people undergo this operation, I realised that it was pretty heroic surgery. I must have been a bit shocked by the news because, afterwards, I lost my way to the chapel, settling instead for a visit to the shop by the exit, and buying a Kit-Kat.

Somewhat later, I sought a second opinion through the Bishops' Doctor, and was directed to Mark Feneley FRCS, at University College Hospital, London (UCH), a leading centre for the treatment for lower pelvic conditions. The excellent urology department at UCH now has a dedicated hospital in Westmoreland Street. I cannot speak too highly of the treatment, care, kindness, openness and – at times – the laughter that they provided, and I am delighted that half of the profit from this memoir will go to them for urological research. I underwent some six short operations under general anaesthetic over four years, mainly to take biopsies; I also had a course of the BCG vaccine which provokes in the bladder a reaction that triggers the immune system to destroy cancer cells. After eighteen months of a three-year course, I had made such good progress that the treatment was suspended. They are continuing with the six-monthly cystoscopies, and occasional scans and biopsies and other treatment to ensure I remain free of cancer.

I really do not know how the hospital manages to do so much with such limited financial resources. In common with many others, I would willingly pay additional tax to bring the country up to, at least the European average (if not maximum) on health care, while continuing the maximum efficiency we see in today's National Health Service.

2013. Confirmation Eucharist at Willesden.

This brief account of my cancer diagnosis underlines the importance of immediate action once we suspect there might be a problem. If there is any uncertainty about the appropriateness of the course of treatment that has been prescribed, a second opinion should be requested, however persuasive those making the initial diagnosis may have been. One in three people receive a cancer diagnosis at some time; there is a huge variety of treatment available, and many survive it. Whatever happens, the patient will be supported and cared for at every turn. From time to time, it is natural to ask oneself the question, 'will this be curtains for me?' - I even did so during an Easter Day Eucharist, as I was beginning the Eucharistic Prayer, when I asked myself, 'maybe next Easter I will be in that place where sacraments have ceased?' We begin to live with such thoughts and - with God's grace - learn to do so without denial or despair; at the same time, we encounter many 'surprises of the Spirit'. I was blessed in being able to continue my ministry throughout my treatment, often returning to work one or two days after an operation or procedure.

Once Fr. Michael Bailey was settled at All Saints' Sidley, the bishop invited me to move to St. Barnabas' Church in central Bexhill, which had been without a parish priest for nearly three years. I was asked to go for six months, 'to steady the ship' during the long vacancy, but six months became two years. My grandparents had ended their days in a flat close to the church; at that time the Anglo-Catholic scholar, Dr. Hubert S. Box, was the Vicar, and the cathedral-like structure was comfortably full at the main Eucharist on a Sunday. As a young man, I remember having tea with Canon Box in his Vicarage, and his giving me a relic of the habit of St. Bernadette of Lourdes. During that same visit, on the feast of St. Michael and All Angels in 1967, I first attended an *Alternative Services Series 2* Eucharist.

Some thirty-five years later, under Fr. Roger Crosthwaite's dynamic ministry, the church became 'charismatic'; while much changed - with an emphasis on the ministry of healing and ecumenism - the Mass was always at the centre of the life of the Church. There was a real sense of outreach to the Town Centre community; the church opened a café, a soup kitchen and a clothing bank. The ministry to the homeless was impressive – indeed, St. Barnabas' provided a welcome and a home to those challenged in any way, and many of them joined the worshipping community.

After Dr. Crosthwaite's short incumbency, there was a long vacancy, and the parish found it hard to maintain the pace, despite excellent interim support from priests, and from lay people, who continued to be supportive when I arrived - especially the Reader Lynda Lynam and her husband Mark Lynam, and the other churchwarden, Dave Cosgrove, and others too numerous to mention. Ordained ministry was offered, among others, by Fr. Nicholas Burton, who was much involved in the Charismatic Movement; by Padre Colin Gibb, experienced in the ministry of healing; by the Revd. Sister Eileen Wheeler, founder of the Servants with Jesus, who had devoted much of her life in the cause of ecumenism; and by Fr Geoffrey Daniels, who was very supportive on the more traditional side. There were many wonderful people at St Barnabas' who led deeply prayerful lives, with a zeal for evangelisation, to whom I owe a great debt of gratitude.

I have always enjoyed working with those from different traditions; when I enter a parish or other place of ministry, I see it as entering that 'running stream'. St. Barnabas' had become rather unfocused, with a number of the congregation 'doing their own thing'. Working with the congregation, everything needed to be brought together, to be given direction and a vision for the future – bearing in mind that certain features in the parochial landscape were non-negotiable. The majority of the faithful were not at St. Barnabas' because it was an Anglo-Catholic Church, or because of its appeal to an aspiring middle-class Anglican congregation. Rather, the new 'unique selling point' at St Barnabas', was rooted in charismatic expression allied to devotion to the Eucharist. Additionally, there was an impressive ministry to the vulnerable. Throughout my ministry, and especially in Blackburn, I had advocated outreach and ministry to the poor and disadvantaged; at St. Barnabas' there was much of this valuable work going on, but in a rather uncoordinated way.

I had agreed to serve as a voluntary priest-in-charge, on the understanding that I could maintain outside commitments and engagements. I was keen to work with the other clergy, while ensuring that there would be no conflicts over gender and Eucharistic presidency. As I am a bishop, I said I would always be the celebrant when I was present. The issue of the ordination and consecration of women was barely mentioned during my time at St Barnabas'. We just pressed on with the ministry and mission of the church despite our differences, respecting each other.

In addition to Sunday Mass, there was Mass on Tuesday and Friday, and I added celebrations on 'Red Letter Days'. Preaching was particularly important at St. Barnabas', so there was also a sermon on weekdays. It was a good discipline for me to have to prepare something carefully on the day's readings. St Barnabas' had a newly commissioned Reader, Paul Abnett, who often preached on Fridays. One Sunday each month, the Parish Mass included the laying on of hands and anointing for healing. As we were a church with a recently-established charismatic tradition, we had some lively and deeply prayerful songs and choruses; Melanie Osborne, our musical director, also possessed a beautiful singing voice. Doreen Saunders, generous and faithful, would turn out to play the organ, whatever the weather or time of day.

The full liturgy for Holy Week was reintroduced; Stations of the Cross were again used devotionally - in memory of Fr. Philip Ilott (a former parish priest, who was also my immediate predecessor at Mayfield, and his faithful and lovely wife, Margaret, continued to worship there) - and in the great fifty days of

Eastertide we introduced Stations of the Resurrection. There was a commitment to prayer, with frequent vigils of prayer before the Blessed Sacrament often ending with Benediction - these occasions being particularly supported by the charismatic section of the congregation. I was keen that there should be some form of association with the Anglo-Catholic charismatic movement, and Mary Morgan, a deputy warden, attended the annual residential conference of the Movement at High Leigh.

The church had some established prayer groups; occasional teaching sessions were begun; and our Reader offered a sequence of Lent and Advent addresses, which were published. I had the rewarding experience of preparing a group of adults for confirmation, most of whom had come from other denominations or house churches. The bishop very kindly allowed me to confirm them in St. Barnabas' on Pentecost Sunday. I trained two servers, Holly Stevenson and Teresa Hills, as bishop's liturgical chaplains – who would accompany me on outside engagements. The three of us formed a school of prayer towards the end of my time at the church, for which I am grateful - this continues to give me more than I bring to it.

After the introduction and confession at the Sunday Mass, there was an open session, lasting fifteen minutes or more, with songs and choruses, including an invitation to members of the congregation to come forward and 'share a message'. This began to concern me; so, after a while, I would approach one or two people beforehand to speak briefly on the theme of the Sunday. With the liturgy now conformed to Anglican norms - and a few other matters tidied up - I was sufficiently content.

In retirement, dining on The Golden Arrow on the Bluebell Line (Sheffield Park - East Grinstead)

During my two years, I encountered warmth, personal kindness and generosity at St. Barnabas', and, for the most part, there was an openness and respect shown to everybody, and a sense of community – we also had a lot of fun and enjoyed many laughs. I am aware of nobody who was lost from this diverse congregation - except by death - and thankfully we certainly gained a few.

It was clear that we could no longer maintain a cathedral-like edifice. With the congregation and

PCC, we looked at possibilities for sharing the building for the future – in fact, we had looked at this some years earlier, when I was archdeacon. I am afraid one of the few times when my blood pressure was raised was when we met some negative comments about sharing the building. I am entirely convinced that sharing is the right course - an act of witness by the church, presenting St. Barnabas' with real opportunities for service and evangelism. At the time of writing, it looks as if this may be taken forward, and this will also ensure that St. Barnabas' can continue to be a presence in the centre of town and a place of welcome and outreach for the foreseeable future. In the meantime the church is focusing on using its facilities for the homeless and beginning to adapt the building accordingly.

After I had left St. Barnabas', Fr. Michael Bailey, the Vicar of All Saints', Sidley, was appointed priest-in-charge, aided by a priest in his final curacy year. The current staffing situation at St. Barnabas' is that Fr. Stephen Huggins, a former Team Vicar in the town, is 'House for Duty' priest, serving the parish along with Fr. Michael and the curate from All Saints' Sidley.

The years of St. Barnabas' as a 'Catholic charismatic church' were exciting in many ways, but for such an experiment to succeed, there needs to be a real commitment from the whole congregation, and with priests from that unique tradition to staff it. Such an exacting programme with present resources could not be sustained in the longer term. It is pleasing to see that now a new pattern of worship and practice appears to be working well, and new opportunities are being grasped.

Some from St. Barnabas' have questioned whether the charismatic years represented a wrong turning, and that it might have been a mistake to attempt a form of worship that was both Eucharistic and charismatic. I am convinced that God the Holy Spirit will often draw a church community to renew His Church by worshipping Him in fresh ways - perhaps only for a short period. There will have been much rejoicing in the heavenly places at the lives that were touched, the broken who came to know Our Lord's healing touch, and the spiritually and physically hungry who were fed. None of this is ever lost, just as the love that was shared cannot be lost. Jesus has taught us to look at the world through His eyes, and when we do that we see that all we do in Him can never be wasted - rather it is taken up by Him 'and hid with Christ in God'. Just as we sense the instantly-recognisable holiness in some churches as the legacy of earlier generations, so something lingers from those 'charismatic' years at St. Barnabas', deeply marking the life of the parish today.

My hope, when I retired, was that I would be able to spend time with those from whom my previous commitments had largely removed me, and to exercise a ministry of encouragement. Certainly, I have been invited to preach, to teach, to take retreats and quiet days, and to lead pilgrimages. Last year I travelled from Glasgow to the Channel Islands - and many places in between - taking Holy Week and Easter services in

Paris. In the Autumn, I took a group from the Society of St. Wilfrid and St. Hilda to Rome, assisted by Fr. Robert Coates, the Parish Priest of St Augustine's, Bexhill (where I help out quite frequently). I am grateful for my wide and varied retirement ministry, and especially for my base at All Saints', Sidley, where Christine and I are always made so welcome, where I am able to celebrate or concelebrate Mass on any occasion, and where we can share in any of the activities of the parish. We are fortunate to live near All Saints', and, indeed, to have other churches nearby where we also feel at home. I quite often meet retired clergy who complain that they are not happy worshipping in their retirement parishes or that they are not being fully used. My advice has always been to check the local churches before deciding where to settle.

I still attend some meetings, and sit on a small number of committees - and I am beginning, at long last, to learn to say 'no'. I have experienced how easy it is to be drawn into intensive activity in retirement, but I know I must now do 'other things' – and this I have managed, to an extent. I have found time to visit family and friends, to read the ecclesiastical and political biographies that I have always enjoyed, to enjoy short breaks, to be pulled by steam engines (including The Flying Scotsman), to take a newspaper break at coffee time and tea time, and to take a walk or a bicycle ride most days. As I had to go out some weeks every night, not only as a bishop, but throughout the whole of my ministry, it is another joy of retirement on many nights to stay in. Christine and I have a not inflexible daily programme, which discourages drifting through the week.

*August 2014. Family gathering at my cousin
Justin's farm at Plumpton.*

With London only fifty-nine miles away, it is relatively easy to get up to the capital. One of the great privileges of having been a Lord Spiritual is that I retain access to the House of Lords and the members' facilities, and can sit on the steps to the Throne to listen to debates. I have also much enjoyed meeting up again with members of the House and taking friends to lunch in the Peers and Guests Dining Room.

While I hugely miss the Diocese of Blackburn and the life of an active bishop, Christine and I are both happy in retirement. I am blessed in having a fairly-extensive, but not exhausting, ministry, and also time for a more relaxed life. By the time these words are published, I will be seventy-two years old, and six years into retirement. Inevitably, in most positions I have held, at some time I have asked the question, 'O God, what next?' It is a question we also ask in retirement.

2018. Claire and Walter with Millie and Isabelle at a family wedding.

14   O GOD, WHAT NEXT?

Bishop Mark Green has popped up in my life at several junctures, and I was delighted when, in 1993, he asked to join me in Eastbourne for the second leg of his retirement.   Mark was a wise and perceptive pastor and became a good friend.   He was also one of the finest and most engaging preachers I have heard.   He kindly preached at the silver jubilee of my ordination to the priesthood in 1999 at Christ Church, St. Leonards-on-Sea.   I have quarried some of the questions below from that address, and invited other questions from those who know me well - seeking the aid of my commonplace book in some of my answers.

1.   You mentioned you had quite a strict upbringing and were sent off to boarding school at the age of seven.
Both of my parents had been born at the beginning of the First World War, and were brought up strictly, and both of them went to boarding school.   They were very caring parents, and from the age of twelve I had a particularly warm relationship with my father.   My mother was very loving and had great energy and could be rather mercurial.

2.   Did you come from a keen church family?
Both my parents had been confirmed at school.   They listened to our prayers every night and we said grace before and after meals.   From the time I was eleven, they seldom missed church.   When I decided I wanted to test my vocation they gave me every encouragement.

3. What has been your regular pattern of devotion?

In addition to Sunday worship, I have attended Mass almost daily for much of my ministry. The daily Office is obligatory for clergy, of course. Before reciting the Office, I find time for other intercession and thanksgiving, meditation and contemplation, including, in the evening, a period of brief reflection on the past day, and the ways God has been at work in my life - as well as the times I have shut Him out. I have always had a spiritual director, availed myself regularly of the sacrament of reconciliation (confession), and made an annual retreat.

4. Would you follow the same pattern of worship, work, and study if you were beginning today?

In essence, what I have outlined is the pattern we observed at the College of the Resurrection, Mirfield. I am a Priest Companion of the Fraternity of the Resurrection, and also an Episcopal Associate in the Society of the Holy Cross. This pattern is also part of my rule of life. It has been my anchor, and I am so thankful to have acquired it at Mirfield. I believe faithfulness to spiritual duties is our absolute priority. Clearly such a daily commitment could not, and should not, be undertaken by most lay people. While it is surely necessary to find some space for prayer, a life of faith for working people with growing families cannot revolve around slipping off at intervals somewhere to recite an Office. Praying is as deep and personal as breathing. Within our hearts God has placed a prayer, and just as we are only aware of our breathing when we pay attention to it, equally we are only aware of praying 'at all times' when we pay attention to it. We cannot forget that we can only 'pray all the time' if we pray some of the time - however limited that time may be.

5. Should you have been stricter about taking time off?
Yes. I have always insisted that clergy take time off and have their holidays. Under the Clergy Terms of Service Measure, 2009, holidays and weekly time off are stipulated. I was quite disciplined about taking holidays, but regret I did not lead by example over the weekly day-off. While we all need time for recreation, priesthood is a way of life and not a job, and a priest is a priest all the time, whatever he is doing. It is often difficult to distinguish between work and leisure. For most of my ministry, I had more than one area of responsibility, and so experienced a great variety of activity; also, I am stimulated by others, and I did not always require a full day-off. I preferred to pace myself, rather than working frenetically in order to ensure a full day-off. For me it was a question of doing what worked best.

6. What advice would you give to those who struggle with prayer?
Don't give up. Much of prayer is like sentry duty - it is a discipline. The time, above all, when we put our trust in God, and open out hearts for Him to do His work in us, can be when prayer becomes a bit of a struggle. It could be that if we do not find prayer difficult we have not started to pray. Prayer is not all about warm and cosy feelings (although they may come) - it is much more about our desire to be close to the heart

of God. I frequently feel my prayer time has been dry and my mind was all over the place. Should that happen to you, do not worry, because the Holy Spirit, who prays in us, is always successful. St. Theresa of Avila said of those wandering thoughts, 'Let the mill clack on while we grind our wheat' - making the point that prayer does not happen in the head, but in the heart. For many years I pinned a card up in my study which summarises for me what prayer is: 'God wants us to let Him love us'.

7. What holy places have been particularly special to you?
For me, any place where the Blessed Sacrament is reserved, is a special place for prayer. All the churches in which I served were special holy places. I have been to the Shrine at Walsingham at least once a year throughout my years of ordained ministry. The Community Church at Mirfield, and the 1966 re-ordered chapel at the Hostel of the Resurrection (now no longer a chapel) were places in which I felt confident that God was at work, constantly inviting me to listen to Him.

I always felt very much 'at home' in the Cathedral at Blackburn, particularly on the cathedra (bishop's chair), looking down to the west-end wall, with John Hayward's dramatic sculpture of 'Christ the Worker'. Praying before that was, for me, powerful.

8. You spoke out a lot on issues of social justice, and some saw you as a 'left-wing' bishop, yet you have not

focused a great deal on that involvement in the book.
Involvement in the community runs through the whole
book, although I acknowledge that I have not gone
into much detail or given many specific examples of
this interest. I could, in particular, have made fuller
mention of this in the Blackburn chapters; but, for
the most part, this was work I did with others. I was
proud of the way the diocese stood up for justice, and
worked against poverty. Of course, we tried with our
limited resources and contacts to care for the victims
of injustice, but I believe we also drove a spoke into the
wheel of much injustice. What began to concern me
greatly - especially in more recent years - is the way we
seem to be normalising poverty and deprivation. We
no longer appear to be shocked – and food banks, for
example, are now a normal part of a town's landscape.
I know the press picked up on the 'left-wing' bishop tag,
but then that usually happens when any bishop speaks
up for the poor and marginalised. Interestingly, one
popular national newspaper described me as 'A Man
of the Right.'

*9. The bishop you served under for the longest period
of time was Dr Eric Kemp and you clearly had a great
admiration for him.*
I did. His ministry spanned much of the twentieth
century, and he embodied for me what the Church
of England could be, at its best. He was certainly shy,
and, appropriately, his memoirs carried the title, 'Shy,
but not Retiring'. No one would call him charismatic,
in the way that term is used today. He was a good
pastor, a fine administrator with a very clear mind, and

certainly one of the wisest people I have ever come across.

He was among the last of the great scholar bishops in the twentieth-century church, and was the author of over sixty books, articles and papers. While he was not always easy to listen to, there was always benefit in reading his words afterwards. I think, particularly, of his Chrism Eucharist addresses; the 'Bishop's Letter' in the *Chichester Diocesan News*; his presidential addresses to the Diocesan Synod; and the booklet of his sermons preached on the occasion of the tenth anniversary of his episcopal ordination, *Joy in Believing*. In 1980, Archbishop Donald Coggan invited him to write the Archbishop of Canterbury's Lent book, which came out under the title *Square Words in a Round World* (1980, Collins Fount Paperbacks). It is a very clear summary of the faith of the Church - with chapters on creation, sin, redemption, the church, life, prayer and communion - and I return to it regularly. Bishop Eric's addresses, lectures, books, and - I understand - boxes of his manuscripts, have been lodged at Lambeth Palace and the West Sussex Record Office.

In an episcopate lasting over twenty-five years and ending when he was eighty-six, and with the huge changes that took place in the Church and in society, Eric understandably made his mistakes - as we all do, and as much younger bishops certainly do. However, the diocese and the Church of England were richly blessed to have a bishop of such wisdom, scholarship, wide experience and holiness at the centre of its life.

At present there appears to be less interest in historical research in the Church, except in limited areas. I suspect when we return to a serious study of the history of the Church, Bishop Eric will emerge as one of the key figures in the Church of England in the twentieth century.

10.   Throughout your ministry you have worked constructively with those from differing traditions: however, the orthodox Catholic group in the Church of England appears to have been increasingly marginalised, particularly in recent decades – do you agree, and how do you feel about this?

Yes, we have been on the margins (but not altogether forgotten), and, as mentioned earlier, the margins are often places where growth springs up – and, right now, that could be a fertile and exciting place to be. One reason that I had a great respect for the late Bishop Eric Kemp is that he gave the Catholic wing real confidence, but also made clear the Catholic nature of the Church of the England, and could always point to documents, reports, conferences and statements which have continued to uphold that position. While there are some very encouraging signs of bright young Anglo-Catholic priests, it will be a while, I suspect, before we see the heavyweight scholar-pastors we saw in the past in the Catholic Movement.

I also question whether the 'smorgasbord' approach to theology and its tradition in the Church of England has helped. In the past, no theological position enjoyed the upper-hand, but now it is generally more of a liberal-catholic-evangelical approach rolled into one. Most certainly, with the consecration of women bishops and other current matters under consideration, orthodox Catholics have suffered a huge blow. If we believe in the revealed faith, and that doctrine can develop - through being more profoundly understood and expressed, *but not changed* – then it does appear to Catholics that much of the Church of England and Anglican Communion is beginning to compromise on the things you just cannot compromise on. That is certainly cause for concern.

We acknowledge that orthodox Catholics have been on the back foot for at least the last twenty-five years, but we are now in a much stronger position. Some good things are happening in our parishes up and down the country, and we are giving a positive lead with work among young people, and in mission and evangelism and ministry to the poor – with 68% of our parishes coming within the most deprived 25% of parishes nationally. With the creation of The Society – under the patronage of St. Wilfrid and St. Hilda - and with Bishops of The Society providing episcopal oversight for priests of The Society and in the 425 parishes who have affiliated to The Society, we have, at last, a proper ecclesial structure. Of course, it is not ideal in every respect, but let us not engage in that favourite Anglican sport of pulling the scrum down by arguing over process. With the Society and 'The House of Bishops Declaration on the Ministry of Bishops and Priests' (2014) with the 'Five Guiding Principles', we are in a more stable position than we were before. The fifth guiding principle states 'Pastoral and sacramental provision for the minority within the Church of England will be made without specifying a limit of time and in a way that maintains the highest possible degree of communion and contributes to mutual flourishing across the whole Church of England'. Thankfully, there are many signs that the Church of England as a whole is directing its energy away from arguing about our differences and focusing on our mission to a post-Christian nation.

11. How can orthodox Catholics contribute to the life of the whole Church – and what more generally is their future?

Much of this question has been answered above. Be positive. We have a more secure future, and I see no need to leave the Church of our baptism. More Catholics could and should become the leaders again. We have, as stated above, some gifted and outstanding priests, and parishes that are 'show cases'. We are located where we are most needed, and happily beaver away, meeting all the challenges. We have some great teachers and evangelists, and, in time, we will surely have some of our priests in positions of considerable responsibility in the Church. Our leaders teach clearly that mission is not just what the Church does, but something that the Church is, reminding us that there are two parts to Our Lord's great commission, 'Go therefore and *make disciples* of all nations, baptizing them in the name of the Father, and of the Son and of the Holy Spirit, *teaching them to obey everything I have commanded you.*' We also need to serve in a positive way, as the ecumenical conscience of the Church of England, and that includes keeping close to others of orthodox faith and life. To this end, it is hoped there will be some serious follow-up to the excellent April 2018 Oxford conference, 'The Gospel and the Catholic Church: Anglican Patrimony Today.'

12. You are usually clear about your stance especially on matters relating to the Faith of the Church, yet you are not 'seriously' partisan and stand in the gap and appear to have an understanding of other's positions.

I suspect that a community of the completely like-minded would not point to the Kingdom of Heaven. I am not quite sure what 'good disagreement' means, but, provided it is not advocating compromising with truth, I hope this is what I strive for. I do favour discussion and dialogue rather than coming to the conversation with a revolver in my belt. I believe, too, if you want to be a conciliator you have to stand in the gap between your position and others who occupy a difference stance. Surely, the bishop is called to be a listener who is with the people. I have had little or no difficulty working with priests and others who have been on the opposite side of the argument on recent controversial issues in the church. Why should I? We believe in the lordship of Christ. We have all subscribed to the Declaration of Assent. There is respect between us. I do not gain my insights exclusively from those who stand with me or learn only from them. My brother-in-law, Canon David Jasper (who is also Professor Emeritus of Literature and Theology at Glasgow University and a parish priest) is a liberal theologian with a great love of sacred scripture and respect for the tradition, but he pushes the boundaries further than I am prepared to do. Nevertheless, I agree with him on so much. In one of his more recent books, he wrote as follows: 'A church without serious theology and a deep sense of prayer should shut up shop today. I have no idea what the Church of tomorrow may actually be like as an institution. But it will survive only if it shuns the material and economic categories of the world, ceases from its anxieties to be seen to be useful or efficient, and lives with all care and precision the life of prayer and service in hidden ways. At the end of Christendom, the Church may learn at length the blessings of obscurity.'

Many traditional Catholics see little point in entering into dialogue with other groups such as liberal Catholics, affirming Catholics, and the Society of Catholic Priests. So long as the temptation is not there to conquer the other side, but to look at ways of working together and 'mutual flourishing', I think, and have found, such contact to be enriching.

13. Do you see hope of greater unity among the churches?

I have written at some length about unity in earlier chapters. Much is going on locally. Just to name a very few examples where there is co-operative working: food banks, churches engaging with other faith communities, street pastors, homeless shelters, and clothing banks. It is open to us, too, to worship in each other's churches. As I write, the Third Anglican-Roman Catholic International Commission (ARCIC III) has issued a statement on how the two churches might learn from one other. The title is, 'Walking Together in the Way: Learning to be the Church – local, regional, universal'. Sadly, with some of the diversions the Anglican Communion has taken in the last forty years, the journey towards unity seems longer and harder than it was when we set out over fifty years ago. Over that time, ARCIC I and II have 'banked' some real agreements and brought the two communions much closer together. Let us pray earnestly that ARCIC III will prove to be ground-breaking, and none of the (in my view) unfortunate paths we have taken will render the existing agreements unsafe. The Holy Spirit has gone before us in our moves towards greater unity with the Roman Catholic, Orthodox and Free Churches, and we have faith that He will build on those relationships and bring us to greater unity.

Picture of me and the Pope, October 2013.

*14. You have voiced some concerns about the current
state of the Church of England.*

There are no complaints to be made about the
professionalism and care provided by the staff in the
National Church Institutions; the Diocese of Blackburn
and I were well supported by them, and by our own
hard-working Church House staff. Although there
is much in the institutional church that is a cause for
concern, I always advise people not to become unduly
worried about that. The institutional church is not itself
the saving community, the Body of Christ; but it can
become disturbingly confused with the Church, the sign
and sacrament of the Kingdom. One has to wonder,
therefore, how well this distinction is understood. I
would argue that most of the Anglican Communion
have already made a change to the sacrament of holy
orders. Parts of the Communion have changed the
sacrament of holy marriage, and now there is serious
talk about changing the sacrament of reconciliation
(confession and absolution) through priests being
ordered to break the seal of the confessional and
having to report abuse of children and vulnerable
adults to the public authorities. Yet again, we are trying
to change – or compromise – on something given to
the Church which we do not have the authority to
change. The seal is non-negotiable. Abuse is a grave
sin, in all circumstances. But, what might happen if the
seal of the confessional could be broken with regard to
a particular sin or sins, and penitents reported to the
police? I doubt whether any would continue to come
to this sacrament, which was given to the Church by
the Risen Lord on the first Easter Day. The sacrament

could no longer be seen as confession to Christ, and, if the seal could be broken for one sin, what would prevent something else leaking? Equally, if penitents continued to come, they would simply omit any sin for which they could be reported, and a vital pastoral and safeguarding opportunity would be missed. It must surely be known that if a penitent confesses to a grave sin, such as murder or abuse, the priest would point out that there is a duty also to admit this to the police, and absolution would be conditional upon this person reporting to a police station. I would also offer to accompany the person to the local police after the sacramental encounter. I fear those who recommend dropping the seal of the confessional in any circumstances neither understand the theology of the sacrament of reconciliation, nor appreciate that this could also be an opportunity to urge someone to report their offence to the police.

15. If you felt you had to leave the Church of England, where would you go?
With the provision of The Society and a life-time of living the Catholic life in the Church of England, I sincerely hope that day will not come. And, after all, I - and The Society - have not compromised on what the Church has received. While I can understand why many have left the Church of England over the past three decades, I have been helped in staying because I am basically a 'Both-And' person – rather than 'Either-Or'. If the day ever dawned when I had to leave, I would be mindful that the Church of England is rooted historically in the Roman Catholic Church, and that

for much of the twentieth century - particularly the last fifty years - we have been in serious dialogue with that Church. Accordingly, I would continue my pilgrimage of faith with my Roman Catholic brothers and sisters, with whom I feel comfortable, and with whose theology I have little difficulty.

16. The greatest pastors have always clothed holiness in garments of humanity and usually humour. Hasn't humour always been important to you?
That is true, and I wish I were among those pastors. I think humour is most important, and a real gift, that can help us to make wise decisions. It stops us taking ourselves too seriously, helps us put things in proportion, and works wonders in reducing the temperature at a meeting. What a grace it is when we can laugh at ourselves. I often feel humour helps us to see the world through God's eyes, because He sees beyond what we see.

17. You have a great respect for Bishop George Bell and have expressed concerns about how the allegation made against him has been handled by the Church of England.
Yes indeed - and I am joined in this by many from around the world. Others much better qualified than me to make a judgement have taken the view, from the earliest stages of the allegation, that the evidence was not compelling. I have yet to meet anyone, anywhere who has looked at the facts available and believes that the handling of this allegation reflects credit on the Church. One comment was 'what a circus' - which

would be amusing if the case were not so serious. It has of course, been extremely difficult to find out much about it, because of the lack of transparency.

To be fair to those who have dealt with this, and in the light of the public reaction, Lord Carlile, QC was invited to review how the Church handled the whole matter. His report leaves the Church with the very difficult task of ensuring that we will never again allow such an injustice to occur. I am surprised the Church did not understand that any institution seeking to act as investigator, accuser, judge and jury cannot deliver justice. I came across a memo, and I cannot remember where it came from, of what Lord Woolton said to Bishop George Bell on 9 February, 1944, just before he made his courageous speech against the indiscriminate bombing of German cities, 'George, there isn't a soul in this House who doesn't wish you wouldn't make the speech you are going to make ... you must know that. But I also want to tell you that there isn't a soul who doesn't know that the only reason why you make it, is because you believe it is your duty to make it as a Christian priest.' That is the Bishop Bell we will all remember, along with his many other heroic deeds. It is tragic, as the Bell Group Press Release of 15 December 2017 argued, that the institutional church today deprived this bishop, who has been dead for over sixty years, of the presumption of innocence or of due process...'.

The Archbishop of Canterbury and the Bishop of Chichester have faced severe criticism for the way in which this whole matter has been handled, and tendered their apologies for it. Lord Carlile QC, who conducted the 2017 independent investigation into the Bishop Bell allegations, forwarded a statement to be read out at the Bell Society meeting on 4 February 2019 in the building that used to be called Bishop Bell House, Chichester. It contained the following words: '*I hope that this event will add to the clamour for the Church to admit the awful mistakes it has made in dealing with unsubstantiated allegations against Bishop Bell. His name should never have been publicised before allegations were investigated. The Church should now accept that my recommendations should be accepted in full, and that after due process, however delayed George Bell should be declared by the Church to be innocent of the allegations made against him.*' With the dedication of the Bishop Bell statue in Canterbury Cathedral (where he served as Dean between 1924 and 29), it is to be hoped that a line may be drawn under this sad episode, banishing any shadow over Bishop Bell's good name - for surely, his character and all he achieved by the grace of God are conjoined.

18. *Is your message really 'Back to the Future'?*
Not at all. My concern is that we dare not neglect what we have received, for if we do so, we will start to look for something new by simply following public opinion - particularly the prevailing view in the country - not least, so that we can be seen as 'relevant' in the eyes of the general public. This surely begs the question,

'Do we prefer the bosom of the state to the bosom of Abraham?' I am not saying that orthodoxy cannot develop, but it must be able to satisfy the test of Vincent of Lerins, who said, 'We hold that faith which has been believed everywhere, always and by all.' Move away from that, and we begin to 'salami slice' away at the received tradition.

I find the received Faith is not actually the problem with young people, just how we apply it! While they are not just the church of the future, they are with us, the church of the present moment, and should be involved appropriately in all levels of church life. The Eucharist has been rightly described as a 'toast to the future with Christ' and the Church, the pilgrim people of God will lead us all into that future. While we cannot deny many of the young are untouched by the church, we do see many examples of their keen involvement and real signs making a difference where we are open and welcoming. They look for what is authentic, and not superficial religiosity, and find it in a community where Jesus Christ and the power of His Resurrection is at the centre. They look for where the action is, and where the Church is a true vehicle of peace, justice and forgiveness and has the courage to break out of our committees and confront the conflicts of our time. They look to the future, and so must we, for it is only as we long for the kingdom, and hunger for that life, that Jesus will transform us into His own life.

I am often asked how I cope in this very broad church,

with my frequent concerns at the direction it is taking. Archbishop Geoffrey Fisher (1887-1972), the ninety-ninth Archbishop of Canterbury, reminded us that it has always been the case that the Church of England has no teachings of her own but the teachings of the Catholic Church. There are also real saints in our tradition, we have faithful congregations all over the country – and throughout the Anglican Communion worldwide. We can be prophetic, we give a real lead in mission; we have had – and still have – many fine theologians, writers and teachers, and all this is just the beginning. My confidence in the Church of England was summed up by Archbishop Rowan Williams in late 2017 in his sermon at the Funeral Mass of our friend and colleague, Bishop Geoffrey Rowell (Bishop in Europe 2001-13). He said of Geoffrey that the good reasons for being Anglican were constantly at the forefront of his mind and his ministry; 'They were part of that deeply Tractarian identity which, for many people, he himself represented. Because part of the Tractarian DNA is, to put it very bluntly, an assumption that the Church of England is always perfectly likely to let you down, and that this is not the end of the world, because Jesus Christ is the Resurrection and the Life. In a time of what you might think is confusion, or even unfaithfulness, dig down, nourish yourself more fully, but be prepared for the personal cost.'

19. *O God what next?*
This is difficult. As the saying goes, 'If you want to make God laugh, tell Him your plans.' It has been an

active retirement ministry so far, and I am happy about that, especially as it has not been to the exclusion of time with family and friends, leisure activities and going away. I am content with my present commitments, helping out where needed and responding to invitations. I hope that mine is, and may continue to be, a ministry of encouragement. Perhaps I should throttle back a little from some involvements, and find more time for listening to God - reading those books on my shelves that have been waiting to be opened for some time, and focusing a bit more on God's passion for justice and equality. As one approaches the evening of life, I need to heed Archbishop Michael Ramsey's advice in a letter he sent to someone recently retired, 'after immense activity one passes into a phase where passivity is the only way. I pray that you may be finding this passivity as the way in which the soul serves God, not by doing this or that but by passively receiving the great stream of His love and compassion.'

20. And then – what next?
The end of the first stage of life. This is the 'where' our current pilgrimage brings us to. I pray that when the time comes for the next stage, I may be able to say, like a recent Bishop of Rome, 'my bags are packed, I am ready to go'. If we do not believe in the Resurrection of the Body and the Life Everlasting, there is surely no sense to be made of the Christian faith. Jesus Christ has shown us that love is stronger than death and given us His Spirit to rise with Him. While I long to be 'at home with the Lord', I do fear leaving behind those loved ones who have supported me through life, and

all that I have come to know in this world created and redeemed by Jesus Christ. I believe I will see again those I have loved – and also those I am sorry I have misjudged and hurt – before the face of God. I believe, too, all the joy I have known here will be seen to be just a foretaste of what awaits us in Heaven. This is part of Our Lord's gift to us, made possible by what He did for us on His Cross and through His mighty Resurrection, 'By His death He has destroyed death, and by His rising again He has restored to us everlasting life.' Through His grace and mercy and the prayers of the saints and others here on earth, I pray that I may be made humble enough to see Him as He really is, and thank Him for all that I have seen of Him in others in this life.

Index of Names and Places

Rahner, Karl (Professor) 37
Ralph, Revd. Dr. Richard 1-2
Ramsey, Michael (Archbishop of Canterbury) 37, 48-9, 50, 53, 82, 97, 194-5, 266
Reade, Charles (father) 3, 5-6, 9, 20, 22, 71, 136, 247
Reade, Christine (née Jasper) 34, 39-40, 45, 48, 66, 74, 82, 96, 100, 105, 127-8, 141, 162, 182, 183, 213, 216-19, 225-6, 244-5, 246, see also Jasper, Christine
Reade, Claire (daughter) 66, 67, 82, 90, 96, 107, 108, 127-9, 152, see also Featherstone, Claire
Reade, Eileen (mother) 3, 4, 5, 6, 9, 129, 247
Reade, Gillian (sister; married Maurice McMahon) 3, 4, 6, 9, 211
Reade, Jeremy (brother) 3, 6, 9
Reeve, Arthur Stretton (Bishop of Lichfield) 43-4
Rice, Condoleezza (US Secretary of State) 180
Rich, Canon Chris 161
Richardson, Paul (Assistant Bishop of Newcastle) 152
Robinson, John (Bishop of Woolwich) 17
Robinson, Tony (Bishop of Wakefield) 198
Rodwell, Revd. Prof. John 24
Ross, Canon Kenneth 56
Rowell, Dr. Geoffrey (Bishop in Europe) 91, 231, 265
Runcie, Dr. Robert (Archbishop of Canterbury) 80, 82, 98

St. Augustine, Bexhill 244
St. Barnabas, Bexhill 236-43
St. Chad, Coseley 43-58, 59, 66, 152
St. Dunstan, Mayfield 4, 87-8, 90-107, 110
St. James, Lower Gornal 69
St. James, Salt 20, 56
St. James, Wednesbury 103-4
St. Mark, Little Common 3-4
St. Mary's Old Town (Eastbourne) 108-35
St. Michael, Bexhill 9
St Nicholas, Codsall 62-3
St. Peter, Upper Gornal 67-89, 93, 102
St. Stephen, St. Peter Port 16
Sandown School, Bexhill 8
Saunders, Doreen (organist) 239
Saville, Revd. Canon Ed (Social Responsibility Officer) 190
Scott-Joynt, Michael (Bishop of Winchester) 14
Scrine, Revd. Ralph (chaplain to Elizabeth College) 14-15, 17-18
Seagrove, Jenny 101
Seed, Kathy 162
Sentamu, Dr. John Tucker Mugabi (Archbishop of York) 224, 225
Shepherd, David (Bishop of Liverpool) 154
Shields, Canon Michael 150
Sidley, All Saints Church 10-11, 14, 230-2, 242, 244
Simmons, Fr. Eric, CR 24
Simper-Watts, Canon Rachel 157
Skelton, Kenneth (Bishop of Lichfield) 59, 82, 88-9
Sloane, Dr. Herbie (army medical officer) 7
Sloane, Maybeth 7
Smith, Chris (Chief of Staff to Archbishop of Canterbury) 200
Smith, Dorothy (archdeacon's secretary) 148
Smith, Preb. Gilbert 58, 60-3

Index created by Meg Davies